THE ILLUSTRATED ATLAS OF HAWAII

The
Illustrated ATLAS

Edited by O. A. Bushnell

*Text by Gavan Daws, O. A. Bushnell,
and Andrew Berger*

*Illustrations by Joseph Feher, Martin Charlot,
Bjorne Skrimstad, and Rogelio Suga*

An Island Heritage Book

of HAWAII

The Illustrated Atlas of Hawaii

Produced by
Island Heritage Publishing

Thirteenth Printing - 1989
Copyright © 1970 Island Heritage Publishing
Library of Congress Catalogue Card No. 70-152566
ISBN 0-89610-034-0
All rights reserved

Please address orders and editorial
correspondence to:
ISLAND HERITAGE PUBLISHING
A Division of The Madden Corporation
99-880 Iwaena Street
Aiea, Hawaii 96701
Phone: (808) 487-7299

Printed in Hong Kong

Introduction

Herald with Conch

The Pacific Ocean is enormous — more than 10,000 miles north to south, more than 10,000 miles east to west at its widest. In area it is more than 70,000,000 square miles, by far the biggest single feature of the globe.

Polynesia, of which the Hawaiian Islands form a part, occupies an area roughly triangular in shape. South of the equator, the extremities of the triangle are New Zealand in the west and Easter Island in the east. Hawaii is the third extremity, north of the equator in the vicinity of the Tropic of Cancer.

This location, more than 2,000 miles from the nearest point of the American continent, more than 2,000 miles from the nearest major island group to the south, makes the Hawaiian Islands the most isolated archipelago in the world. This, together with the fact that the total land area of the Hawaiian chain is less than 6,500 square miles, makes it understandable that discovery and settlement by a native population did not take place until late in the world's history—on the evidence, perhaps as late as the eighth century A.D.

Westerners came upon Hawaii for the first time something like a thousand years later—in the eighteenth century. It was immediately obvious to the white men that the Hawaiians were physically and culturally related to islanders in other parts of the Polynesian triangle south of the equator. Equally clearly, Polynesians as a whole were different from the other broadly recognizable groups of islanders in the Pacific, Melanesians and Micronesians.

Considering the vastness of the Pacific, and the enormous difficulty experienced by white men in sailing it and plotting the positions of the principal islands—a process that took them more than 250 years—the achievement of the Polynesians in locating and peopling their islands could only be described as remarkable. Their

origins and their migrations among the islands of the great triangle have always been matters for speculation. Scholars and scientists have tried—and are still trying—any number of ways to get at the facts, but even now a good many matters remain unexplained.

The Polynesians themselves had an elaborate tradition of their origins and history, maintained in religious, genealogical and narrative chants. During the nineteenth and twentieth centuries, a good many traditions were set down in writing by interested white men and by natives with a Western education, and scholarly studies have been made, reconciling the traditions of one island group with those of another, and trying to connect the traditions of Polynesia as a whole.

Often it was possible for scholars to put together a likely sequence of historical events, but to assign a reliable Western chronology was difficult, because the Polynesians dated events no more exactly than by generations or by the reigns of chiefs. Accordingly if, for example, a generation was taken by a scholar to be 25 years on the average, rather than 30, an event mentioned as taking place 20 generations in the Polynesian past could be located only in a given century, not in a particular year or even a particular decade.

This kind of difficulty reappears in studies of the Polynesian language itself. It is possible to make an extensive list of words common to all of Polynesia, and to note how in different island groups a word retains its meaning but changes its pronunciation. With a sufficiently large body of evidence, it would be possible to make hypotheses about the length of time the population of one island group had been separated from another, giving these changes time to develop. And from this, other hypotheses might be made about the direction of migration. But again, this useful linguistic work does not yield precise results in historical terms.

Physical anthropologists have studied the skeletal remains of ancient Polynesians, and have compared them with the physiques of modern-day Polynesians, in the hope of determining relationships within Polynesia, and with other parts of the Pacific. Parallel studies have been made in serology, to determine the occurrence of different blood types among modern islanders, again in an effort to learn something of their origins, dispersal, and eventual groupings. Again the results have been useful but inconclusive.

The science most likely to solve the Polynesian puzzle—if indeed a solution is possible—is archeology: the systematic study of plant, animal and human remains recoverable in historical sequence above and below ground in the islands. Archeological work of permanent usefulness is relatively recent in Polynesia—its beginnings are only a few decades in the past—and a great deal more work is needed. But already the outlines of the migrations that settled Hawaii from south of the equator are much clearer than they have ever been, and the larger question of the general origins of the Polynesians is being attacked with encouraging results.

Contents

POLYNESIAN ORIGINS AND MIGRATIONS

The first Hawaiians came from south of the equator, from the Marquesas Islands and the Society Islands of central Polynesia. But where did the central Polynesians come from in turn? Archeological findings, together with studies of winds, currents, flora and fauna, suggest that the origin of the Polynesian culture was in the western Pacific.

Linguistic studies support this idea. The vocabulary of the Polynesian islanders is related to a widely dispersed language family extending west across Southeast Asia—as far west, indeed, as Madagascar.

Current theory suggests that the major island complex of Samoa-Tonga is the first place where a distinct Polynesian culture developed. A characteristic physical type and social organization were then spread by migration to develop in specialized ways on widely separated island groups. The Society Islands and neighboring archipelagoes were evidently stepping-off places for migratory voyages to the extremities of Polynesia: Easter Island, New Zealand, Hawaii.

In opposition to this general body of theory and evidence is the work of Thor Heyerdahl, who has devoted a great part of his active life to the idea that the origin of Polynesian culture is not Asian but American. Certain elements of the Polynesian flora and fauna are American in origin, and Heyerdahl's own Kon-Tiki raft expedition demonstrated that human contact was possible between the Pacific coast of South America and Polynesia. But whether America has been a main element in the emergence of Polynesian culture, or merely subsidiary, or indeed no more than a problematic presence, remains an unresolved question. The weight of available evidence, as indicated, favors an Asian origin.

As far as the narrower question of the immediate origin of Hawaiian culture is concerned, archeological findings, including dating of material by radio-carbon techniques, have now made it possible to say with some certainty that the first permanent settlements were made by migrants from the Marquesas Islands in about the eighth century A.D., and that subsequent migrations from the Society Islands between the eleventh and fourteenth centuries A.D. established the culture which, in a developed form, was brought to Western eyes by the discoveries of white explorers in the late eighteenth century.

Quite apart from the question of origins, the navigational techniques of the Polynesians have fascinated Westerners. Hawaiian traditions, for example, speak of two-way voyages between Hawaii and Tahiti, a distance of well over 2,000 miles of open ocean. What clouds the question is

Great double canoes, joined by a platform bearing a thatched hut, could carry fifty people and their possessions from Tahiti to Hawaii.

that at the time of the Western discoveries, such voyages had ceased, and they were never resumed by the islanders, the old technical knowledge—and perhaps the old confidence—having apparently been lost. White men have tried endlessly to reconstruct, on paper and in practice, the techniques which enabled the Polynesians, without sailing ships of large size and deep draught, and quite without Western instruments and maps, to find for the first time, and then find again, island groups so widely separated.

The big double-hulled, decked and roofed oceanic sailing canoes in which the migratory voyages must have been made were still being used for shorter inter-island voyages when the white discoverers came to Polynesia, and detailed drawings of

them by Westerners survive. In 1976, a scientif[ic] expedition called the Hokule'a, using a 60-fo[ot] canoe built according to ancient Polynesian desig[n] and sailed by traditional Polynesian navigation[al] techniques, journeyed from Hawaii to Tahiti an[d] back, demonstrating the feasibility of such vo[y]ages. On a more theoretical level, computer studi[es] have been made to work out the probabilities [of] success and failure in oceanic voyaging in Polyn[e]sia over a long period of time.

At one extreme of theory is the propositic[n] that Polynesia could have been peopled b[y] random one-way voyages—that is to say, more [or] less accidentally, by castaways, political exile[s] and adventurers. Given enough time, and enoug[h] canoes swept into unknown waters by changi[ng]

Evidence suggests that seafarers from the Marquesas settled near South Point, Hawaii. Unless they arrived fully equipped, they would have had to make at least one voyage home for food plants and animals.

winds and currents, enough survivors would have found new archipelagoes and settled them. This theory, of course, does not really account for the existing traditional evidence of two-way voyaging between an island homeland and a newly-settled archipelago a great distance away. Apart from anything else, two-way voyaging argues a considerable knowledge of astronomy, which obviously would have to be built up over a period of time. Current reconstructions suggest that the Polynesians' astronomical knowledge was serviceable, and that they were extremely skilled sea-goers—as would be expected from their adaptation to life on small islands in a great ocean.

ANCIENT HAWAIIAN SOCIETY

Estimates of the Hawaiian population in the late eighteenth century, the time of the Western discovery, range from as low as about 150,000 to as high as about 400,000. A figure of 300,000 represents the currently agreed-upon educated guess. By then the Hawaiians were well settled on the major islands of the chain—Hawaii itself, the biggest island, Maui, Molokai, Lanai, Kahoolawe, Oahu, Kauai and Niihau.

The characteristic terrain of the islands—rugged inland mountains, with valleys more or less suitable for agriculture leading out to narrow coastal flatlands and coral reefs in the shallow water—encouraged this settlement pattern of small dispersed groups, and probably did something in turn to encourage a political development along tribal rather than unitary lines.

The typical landholding pattern was based on a unit called the *ahupuaa,* ideally a wedge-shaped area of land extending from the mountains to the sea, within which all the necessities of life could be found. The basic occupations were agriculture and fishing. The two staple items of the Hawaiian diet were fish and *poi,* a paste made from the cooked and pounded root of *taro,* grown in the valleys in ingenious and carefully tended irrigated plantations. This diet was supplemented by the meat of pigs, chickens, and dogs, and various fruits, including the coconut and the banana.

The Hawaiian religion bore a general resemblance to that of other Polynesian island groups. Four principal gods, all male—Ku, Kane, Lono and Kanaloa—exercised ultimate jurisdiction over human activity, and countless minor gods and spirit beings were present as forces in the natural world. The gods had created the world and all that was in it. Men going about their daily occupations were constantly aware of this. The calendar of the month and the year was based on ritual observances. The most powerful human beings among the Hawaiians were the high chiefs,

Warriors from Tahiti conquered the pioneer menehune. Taller, stronger, haughtier, claiming the great gods as ancestors, these were the ali'i, the new rulers of Hawaii.

Women of the village making Tapa.

the *alii,* and their priests, who were most closely in touch with the gods. The most imposing structures erected by the Hawaiians were the stone-platformed *heiaus,* or religious temples.

The organizing principle of Hawaiian religion, and of Hawaiian society generally, was that of *kapu* or taboo. There were *kapu* people, places, things, times. They were sacred, and any profanation of their sacredness was held to be extremely dangerous and disturbing to the well-being of individuals and the equilibrium of society. Thus a tremendously involved and detailed code of behavior grew up, regulating the relationships of the individual Hawaiian with his contemporaries, with his ancestors and descendants, and with his natural surroundings, with the world at large.

At the time of the Western discovery, no single chief had control of the whole island chain. Rather, on each island, one or more chiefs of high birth, political talent and military ambition were contestants for power.

War among the competing chiefs was a constant possibility and a frequent actuality. But total war was not feasible. The economy of the islands was basically a subsistence economy, and could not stand long periods of wasteful unproductiveness. By the eighteenth century, evidently, the population had grown to a point where the resources of the islands were beginning to be strained, and extensive destruction and prolonged neglect of agriculture would not have been supportable. Thus, although the ambition of the chiefs was comprehensive, war in practice was confined to sporadic raiding of enemy territory by bands of warriors rather than massed invasions by all able-bodied men.

As long as there was no single conquering chief, the power of all Hawaiian *alii* was limited to some degree. Whether, undisturbed by contact with the West, Hawaiian society would ever have crossed the line from tribalism to some sort of unified primitive state is problematical. Certainly the chances for new experiments in power politics provided by the appearance of white men with an advanced military technology transformed Hawaiian traditional society in the space of one or two generations.

The Hawaiian Islands were the last in Polynesia, and the last major group in the Pacific, to come under the notice of Westerners. This can be explained, once again, by their isolated location in the north central Pacific. Throughout the age of Pacific exploration, from the early sixteenth to the late eighteenth century, Europeans on voyages of discovery characteristically entered the Pacific Ocean in the south, either by rounding the extremities of South America in the east, or by rounding the Cape of Good Hope at the

Hawaii eluded Europe's mariners for 268 years after they entered the Pacific. In 1624-1625 eleven Dutch ships, the "Nassau Fleet," sailed from America to Guam at latitudes too far south to discover Hawaii.

foot of Africa in the west and crossing the Indian Ocean to enter the western Pacific. In either case, the wind and current systems of the southern hemisphere repeatedly made voyages exhaustingly long, thus reducing the opportunities for systematic canvasses of the northern ocean.

The history of exploration in the Pacific reflects the changing imperial fortunes of the European powers. Broadly, the sixteenth century belonged to Spain. The first trans-Pacific voyage, that of Ferdinand Magellan in 1519, was part also of the first circumnavigation of the earth, and it was carried out under the auspices of the Spanish court. Later, Spanish settlements in South and Central America laid a base for voyages between Mexico and Spain's colony in the Philippines.

The presence of Spain's Manila galleons in the northern Pacific for two centuries has led to speculation that the Spanish must surely, at one time or another, deliberately or inadvertently, have located the Hawaiian Islands. There is fragmentary evidence in Hawaiian tradition of the landing of a party of white men at some undetermined time, and attempts have been made by scholars to link this with Spanish records of shipwreck, or expeditions off course. Hawaii would certainly have been a useful discovery for the Spanish. For all this, the historical records of Spain remain silent on the subject. The known track of the Manila galleons took them south of Hawaii on the way from Mexico to the Philippines, and far to the north on the return voyage. Speculation on the subject remains no more than speculation.

As the sixteenth century was Spain's, so in general the seventeenth century in Pacific exploration belonged to the Netherlands. In strict terms they were interlopers in the overseas domains marked out for Portugal and Spain, but Dutchmen on the far side of the earth could not be expected to trouble themselves much on such scores. Their contributions to geographical knowledge came as a by-product of their commercial ventures. Characteristically, they entered the Pacific from the west, and confined themselves for the most part to the western Pacific. Even the voyages of their greatest navigator, Abel Tasman, did not approach Hawaii.

The Spanish were interested in the legendary riches of undiscovered places, and in the salvation of souls among the heathen natives they encountered. The Dutch were more prosaic men of commerce. The eighteenth century brought Frenchmen and Englishmen into the Pacific on voyages of discovery, and here the older motives for exploration were enriched by a genuine and powerful scientific and intellectual curiosity.

The major object of this curiosity was the mythical Great Southern Continent, whose existence had been postulated since classical times by geographers arguing that the land masses of the earth must have a certain symmetry about them, the south matching and balancing the north. At the opening of the modern age of exploration, as far as precise geographical knowledge was concerned, the Southern Continent might well have occupied any part of the southern Indian Ocean or the southern Pacific. Successive voyages by French and English expeditions narrowed down its possible extent. But the tremendous difficulties involved in lengthy Pacific voyages—food shortages, disease, uncertainties about navigational position—left the Continent still a philosophical possibility, if an actual mystery, until the definitive voyages of James Cook.

And as far as the discovery of Hawaii was concerned, continued concentration on the southern Pacific pushed the waters north of the equator into second place. The existence of a major group of islands strategically located there, potentially very valuable to sea-going powers, remained unsuspected.

CAPTAIN COOK'S DISCOVERY

James Cook's first two voyages took him to the South Pacific. He entered the ocean for the first time in January 1769, en route to Tahiti to make astronomical observations of the transit of Venus across the face of the sun. In his secret instructions were provisions for the annexation of the Southern Continent, should he discover it. He did not, and neither did he on his second voyage, 1772-1775, during which he covered between 60,000 to 70,000 miles in southern waters.

If Cook could not find the much-discussed Southern Continent, it did not exist. He was the explorer's explorer—navigator, chart-maker, commander of ships, leader of men without peer, one of the greatest Englishmen of his day. His work gave detailed shape to Western understanding of the South Pacific, and he left only the most minor of discoveries to be made there by his successors.

Two superbly successful voyages such as these encouraged the British government to send Cook on a third, this time to the North Pacific in search of another geographic will-of-the-wisp which had attracted the interest and attention of the European powers for centuries. Cook was to try to find a sea passage from the Pacific to the Atlantic, across the north of the American continent.

His track from the Society Islands to the west coast of North America led him to encounter the Hawaiian Islands. On the morning of January 18, 1778, Cook, with his two ships, HMS *Resolution* and HMS *Discovery*, raised the three westernmost inhabited islands of the chain: Oahu, Kauai, and Niihau.

Cook went ashore at Waimea on Kauai and on Niihau, spending two weeks in provisioning his ships and making a brief study of the Hawaiian people, their land, and their institutions.

Cook named his new discovery the Sandwich Islands, after the First Lord of the Admiralty. On February 2, he left for the American west coast, and spent the better part of 1778 looking in vain for the sea passage. Turning south again to spend the winter in warmer latitudes before making another attempt at the discovery, he brought his ships to the eastern end of the Hawaiian chain, raising the island of Maui on November 25-26, 1778, and the island of Hawaii immediately

Captain James Cook, R.N.
(1728 - 1779)

afterwards. He spent the last weeks of 1778 and the first of 1779 coasting Hawaii. Not until he rounded the island's south point and set off along its west coast did he find what he was looking for: safe anchorage in a well-populated, well-supplied district. On January 17 he put in at Kealakekua Bay with the idea of remaining there for as long as it took to get his ships and men back in good condition for the arduous northern exploratory work that still lay ahead of them.

Cook had come at an important time in the Hawaiian religious year. Both his landfalls, first at Kauai in January 1778, then at Kealakekua in January 1779, took place during a festival known as the *Makahiki*. For the Hawaiians, the god Lono was the deity of agricultural fertility, and it was believed that he made annual visits to his people around the turn of the year. To receive

In l778, iron was so precious to Hawaiians that they offered a large hog in exchange for one English nail.

Honolulu in 1816 was a hot, dirty, dusty village of about 300 grass huts. Its population varied with the number of foreign ships anchored in the tiny harbor of Kou.

him, and to do him honor, the Hawaiians suspended work and war for several weeks at a time, and spent their days in games and feasting, while the image of Lono was carried around the islands and the chiefs and priests collected goods in tribute under Lono's auspices.

In a sense this was highly fortunate for Cook. The Hawaiians, tremendously impressed by the size of his ships and the strangeness of the men and equipment they carried, took Cook to be Lono himself. They heaped honors upon him, and gifts of supplies upon the expedition.

On February 4 Cook left Kealakekua Bay, intending to look at some of the islands between Hawaii and Kauai before going north again a second time. But a storm damaged the foremast of his flagship, HMS *Resolution,* and forced him to turn back to Kealakekua. Arriving there, he found the rejoicing and celebrating crowds of his earlier visit gone. The *Makahiki* was over.

Cook's carpenters took the damaged foremast ashore, expecting repairs to take some days. On the night of February 13, some natives stole a ship's boat from the *Discovery*—a serious theft, and one which Cook could not disregard. He went ashore next morning with a small party of marines, intending to bring the ruler of the island, the chief Kalaniopuu, back to the *Resolution* as a hostage for the return of the boat. As the party was making its way down to the beach, a crowd of natives gathered. The mood of some of Kalaniopuu's warriors turned ugly. There was a scuffle which turned into a fight. Cook's men fired their guns. The Hawaiians attacked, and Cook was struck down and killed at the water's edge.

KAMEHAMEHA THE GREAT

The rise to power of the high chief Kamehameha, who became the first king of the Hawaiian Islands, coincided exactly with the opening of the era of contact with the West. Kamehameha was born in the Kohala district of the island of Hawaii, probably about 1758, though the precise date is unknown. The ruler of the island of Hawaii at that time was Kamehameha's uncle Kalaniopuu, who also controlled the Hana district of eastern Maui. Arranging for the succession in anticipation of his death, he gave his son Kiwalao charge of his lands, and to Kamehameha he gave charge of the highly important god Kukailimoku, who was worshipped to bring success on the battlefield.

Argument and fighting took place over the distribution of land on Hawaii, and it was Kamehameha's success in these local disputes that led him down a path of war which brought him to control of almost the whole island group by 1795.

The great obstacle facing Kamehameha on the islands west of Hawaii was the chief Kahekili, who controlled most of Maui and its neighboring islands, Molokai and Lanai, and had kinship ties with the rulers of Oahu and Kauai. Kamehameha defeated Kahekili's son, Kalanikupule, at the battle of Iao Valley on Maui; but not until after the death of Kahekili in 1794 did Kamehameha invade the island of Oahu. A decisive campaign was fought there in 1795, when Kamehameha led a fleet of canoes and small Western schooners to the southern shores of Oahu, landed, and pressed inland to the valley of Nuuanu, where his men engaged and routed the forces of the heir of Kahekili, Kalanikupule.

With victory at Nuuanu, Kamehameha controlled all the major islands except Kauai and Niihau. He made two attempts to invade Kauai over the years. In 1796 he set out with his fleet of canoes into the Kauai channel, but had to turn back because of rough weather and high waves. And the more substantial fleet he assembled in 1804 to carry his men the length of the chain from Hawaii to Kauai had brought his army only as far as Oahu when an epidemic (a Western disease, probably cholera) struck and decimated his army and the population of the island in general. Eventually, Kamehameha got what he wanted without fighting. In 1810, he reached an agreement with the ruling chief of Kauai that gave him suzerainty over Kauai and Niihau.

Kamehameha's governmental organization was unique in the Pacific. No native chief of his day or later managed so completely to impose his will

Kamehameha I (1758? - 1819)

on an entire island chain—and, for that matter, on the white men who appeared in increasing numbers. To keep the control of the islands in his hands, Kamehameha appointed governors who reported directly to him, men chosen for their loyalty to him, and also for their freedom from kinship ties with the old ruling chiefs. Kamehameha also made it a point of the greatest importance to build up a supply of Western arms, at the same time denying other chiefs the opportunity of collecting guns. The other part of his arrangements which ensured him continued dominance was a royal monopoly of trade, constantly enforced. No chief or commoner was allowed to barter with Western ships on his own account. No Western captain, arriving with his ship, was allowed to begin trade anywhere in the islands without Kamehameha's permission.

Kamehameha II (1797 - 1824)

Cook's expedition did not traffic in arms with the Hawaiian chiefs, and the next Western ship to call at the islands did not appear until 1785. But every year after that ships called, and with increasing frequency. Hawaii became a way-station in a new sea-borne trade linking the northwest coast of America with China. The share of the islands in this trade was simple: the chiefs provided Western ships wintering in Hawaii with food and supplies, and in return they asked for Western goods, with a great emphasis on iron and guns.

The same trade that brought Kamehameha his guns brought a great change in the settlement patterns of the islands. Honolulu harbor was discovered by Westerners, probably in 1794, though again the precise date is unknown. It was the only deep-water harbor in the islands, and the only one, in fact, for thousands of miles. With Western ships putting in there as a matter of course, Honolulu became important enough for Kamehameha to move his court there in 1804.

BREAKING OF KAPUS

Until about 1810, foreign trade remained much the same, with merchant ships calling at the islands for food and supplies. But then a new element appeared: Westerners discovered that the Hawaiian Islands had big stands of sandalwood trees. The aromatic wood was much in demand in China, and accordingly the new trade was added to the old. Again, Kamehameha kept a monopoly, and used some of the proceeds to add to his always-growing collection of foreign ships. The sandalwood trade survived into the 1820s, declining sharply toward the end of that decade with the exhaustion of the sandalwood stands.

After his sojourn at Honolulu (1804-1812), Kamehameha decided to move back to his home island of Hawaii. He had no more need for military campaigning, particularly after his agreement with the ruling chief of Kauai in 1810. And even though Honolulu was rapidly becoming the center of commerce, the king could rely on his governors to supervise trade efficiently.

By this time Kamehameha was an elderly man. He lived out his last years on Hawaii, and died at something like seventy years of age at Kailua on May 8, 1819.

The question of the succession had been settled some years earlier, when Kamehameha named his son Liholiho as his heir. Another question, which could not be settled until the death of Kamehameha made it urgent, was whether the new form of government would survive the disappearance of the unifier.

Kamehameha had been a military conqueror

and a political innovator, but he was always a conservative in matters of religion. In particular he resisted any suggestion from white men that he might give up the old worship in favor of Christianity.

The position of the old religion, however, was no longer secure. In particular, the idea of *kapu* had come into question. In a way, the continuance of the *kapu* system depended on the continued isolation of the islands. Now that isolation was gone, the Hawaiians encountered for the first time a race of people, the Europeans, who could apparently break the *kapus* without punishment by the gods.

Evidently, in the forty years between Cook's visit and the death of Kamehameha, a considerable skepticism about the *kapus* grew up among some Hawaiians, including several of the chiefs.

Kaahumanu and Keopuolani eventually persuaded Liholiho to have a public feast at which women would be permitted to eat with men, and at which foods formerly forbidden to women would be served. This would symbolize the breaking of the *kapus*. The feast was served, the foods were eaten, the *kapus* were broken.

Some conservative chiefs on the island of Hawaii took up arms in November 1819 in defense of the old system, but the armaments of Kamehameha, inherited by Liholiho, were sufficient to stamp out the revolt, and Liholiho remained king.

Ruling as Kamehameha II (1819-1824), Liholiho never really settled down to the task of being a king. To follow such a formidable figure as his father would have been difficult in any circumstances. To lead a people who had just

When the kapus were abandoned, the gods lost their power.

In view of the fact that the *kapu* system discriminated against women in matters of behavior and even in matters of the foods that might safely be eaten, it is perhaps not surprising that when an attack on the *kapus* came, it originated among the female chiefs.

Kamehameha, in the course of his life, had had as many as twenty-one wives. Some of them survived him. The two most important and influential after his death were his favorite wife, Kaahumanu, and the mother of his two sons, Keopuolani. In the months that followed Kamehameha's death, these two began to urge the new king, Liholiho, to flout the *kapus*.

The episode which followed is one of the strangest in the history of the Pacific, or indeed of the world—a people giving up a religious system which had been theirs for centuries, and not replacing it.

The events were simple but momentous.

seen the *kapu* system dismantled was more difficult still. Liholiho, no more than a youth when he became king, found himself unable to control chiefs and commoners as Kamehameha the Great had done in maturity and old age. Restless and indecisive, the new king made only one important decision—to visit Great Britain and perhaps learn something of the art of ruling at the greatest royal court of the day. This was an uncertain venture, to say the least, and it turned out to be fatal. The Hawaiian royal party succumbed to disease in London, and Liholiho and his wife died there, of measles, in July 1824.

MERCHANTS AND MISSIONARIES

Two events during Liholiho's reign set the course of major developments during the reign of his successor, his younger brother, Kauikeaouli,

American missionaries

the last son of Kamehameha the Great, who reigned as Kamehameha III (1825-1854). First, in the fall of 1819, American ships caught a whale off the coast of Hawaii. Second, in the spring of the following year, 1820, American Protestant missionaries arrived in the Hawaiian kingdom. The whaling industry of the northern Pacific, dominated for the next fifty years by firms based on the New England port towns, turned Honolulu on Oahu and Lahaina on Maui into the busiest ports in the Pacific, and tied the economic growth of Hawaii to the United States. The missionary effort in turn was dominated by New Englanders, and was just as important in linking the Hawaiian kingdom with the United States—perhaps more so.

After a great popular religious awakening among the commoners in the late 1820s, as many as 30 percent of the population could be claimed as members of the church by 1853. Without much doubt, the most important white men in the islands during the reign of Kamehameha III were Hiram Bingham, leader of the first missionaries to arrive in 1820; William Richards, who left the mission in the late 1830s to teach the chiefs the rudiments of Western government; and Gerrit Judd, a former missionary doctor who became the chief minister of the government in the 1840s and early 1850s. For such men, inevitably, the idea of useful change among the Hawaiians was to make all the Kingdom's institutions, religious, educational, political, economic, as American as possible.

Beginning in 1838, the ruling chiefs of Kamehameha III began to take instruction in "political economy" from William Richards. In 1839, a declaration of rights was formulated, and in 1840, the first written constitution of the kingdom was framed and promulgated, establishing an elementary representative legislature (which included commoners among its members), setting out the government's executive powers, and inaugurating a supreme court.

Organic laws enacted in the middle 1840s made possible the further development of governmental machinery. A revision of the constitution in 1852 showed further American influence in the broadening of the franchise to something resembling universal male suffrage, balanced, however, by the continued existence of an upper house of hereditary high chiefs and royally appointed "nobles."

Beginning in the middle 1840s, a land commission supervised a series of arrangements known as the Great Mahele or the great division, reapportioning land among crown, government, chiefs and commoners, bringing in for the first time the Western principle of private ownership in land. By 1850 it was possible for a foreigner to purchase land in fee simple.

In all this, as remarked, American influence was strong. Great Britain and France were also interested in the islands of the Pacific, to the point of carrying out annexations in island groups in southern Polynesia. In the reign of Kamehameha III, Hawaii faced threats to its independence from these two powers. More than once, French warships menaced Honolulu, their commanders insisting on the rights of French subjects there (including Catholic missionaries who arrived in 1827 but were unable to establish themselves properly until a declaration of religious toleration was made in 1839). And from February 25 to July 31, 1843, the Hawaiian kingdom underwent a temporary loss of independence when a British naval officer, Lord George Paulet, used the threat of his ship's guns to establish a protectorate on behalf of his home government. Independence was restored when the British Foreign Office disavowed his action.

That Hawaii remained an independent kingdom was in large part due to the attitude of the United States, which in 1841 had declared its interest in the continued existence of the kingdom as a sovereign state. The United States would not permit any other power to annex Hawaii, and would not—for another half-century —be an annexationist power itself.

The California gold rush of the late 1840s operated to create a new economic tie between Hawaii and the west coast of America to match the tie with the east coast created by whaling. After California became a state of the union, expansionist Americans in the islands worked to carry the new tie further: to have the islands annexed by the United States. This in itself would have caused the government of the kingdom great alarm. But in the context of great uncertainty about the possible imperialist ambitions of France, the Hawaiian government went so far as to agree to the secret framing of an annexation treaty with the United States. But there were good reasons in both Honolulu and Washington why the treaty should not have been perfected. As mentioned, the United States was not yet ready for oceanic imperialism, particularly of a kind involving islands with a non-white population. The Hawaiian kingdom, preferring of course not to be annexed at all, was able, after considerable diplomatic maneuvering, to get the United States, Britain and France to agree to support the idea of continued independence for Hawaii.

RISE OF SUGAR

Kamehameha III died on December 15, 1854, leaving no legal heir of his own issue. He was succeeded first by Alexander Liholiho, Kamehameha IV (1854-1863), and Lot, Kamehameha V (1863-1872), brothers from another part of the Kamehameha dynasty. Alexander Liholiho and Lot were politely but strongly anti-republican and anti-American—largely as a result of their observations and experiences during a visit to the United States arranged for them as part of their youthful education by Gerrit Judd. Instead, they took their ideas about the proper form of government and the proper place of royalty from Victorian Britain, and Alexander Liholiho made it a point to invite an Anglican mission to Hawaii, and to be married in an Anglican ceremony.

Once these statements of intent had been registered and assessed, it remained true, whatever the Hawaiian kings did, that the money economy of the islands remained dependent on the United States. And this was so despite what amounted to a radical change in the sources of income for Hawaii. At the start of the reign of Kamehameha IV, whaling was still the principal revenue-earner, with an average of something like 400 whaleships per year arriving in Hawaiian ports during the peak years of 1855-1857.

Whaling went into decline in the 1860s, brought to a low point and then almost to extinction by the discovery of the uses of petroleum in the United States, and by the economic disturbances caused by the Civil War. As whaling diminished in the North Pacific, the relative and absolute importance of the sugar industry to Hawaii increased.

Sugarcane, which grew wild in the islands, had been milled and boiled in a small way as early as

Kamehameha III (1813-1854)

1802 (by a Chinese living on Lanai), and there had been attempts at large-scale plantation culture since the middle 1830s. Expanded cultivation and processing was made possible by the California goldrush, which opened up a substantial market in a very short time. In turn, the end of the rush and the sharp decline in the California market brought a corresponding contraction in the islands.

Once more it was the Civil War that made a crucial difference. Just as the American whaling fleet, operating out of the Northern ports of New England, was disorganized by war, so were the sugar plantations of the South, which had been the big national suppliers. The war thus allowed Hawaiian sugar to make its way into the American mainland market in quantity, replacing the lost Southern sugar.

After 1865, peace threatened this arrangement. To secure the sugar market became a prime point of Hawaiian policy. The surest way would have been to negotiate a treaty of commercial reciprocity with the United States, under which sugar from the islands would be admitted duty-free to the market in the United States, in return for corresponding privileges for certain American goods in the Hawaiian market.

Reciprocity began to be discussed seriously in Hawaii as early as 1848, and during the 1850s and 1860s several attempts were made to bring Congress to the point of considering the proposition seriously as well. Americans living in the islands regarded the idea of reciprocity as advantageous in purely economic terms, and they were not averse to any closer political tie which might be created by a commercial treaty. Hawaiian

kings, chiefs, and commoners could be brought to see the economic point. On the politics of reciprocity, however, they were deeply divided, not being able to decide whether reciprocity would prove useful in staving off annexation by the United States, or helpful in bringing it on.

During a depression which struck the islands in the early 1870s, economic considerations became more pressing than ever, and the Americans in the islands, many of them directly involved in the suffering sugar industry, redoubled their efforts. But not many Americans knew about Hawaii, or felt responsible for her economic welfare. Washington, for its part, was leisurely in discussing the implications of reciprocity, economic and political, and in the end it took until 1875 for the consummation of a treaty, to be put into effect in 1876.

A continuing decrease in the native population caused sugar planters to import workers from Asia and Europe. The first group of contract laborers arrived from China in 1852.

RECIPROCITY

The rise of the sugar industry came at the same time as a drastic and apparently irreversible fall in the size of the native population of Hawaii. Various introduced diseases, the most serious of which were cholera, venereal diseases, smallpox and leprosy, brought the number of native Hawaiians down from an estimated 300,000 at the time Cook visited the Islands to less than 45,000 a century later.

Apart from the possibility that, if this trend were not reversed, the Hawaiian people might soon be on the brink of disappearance, the decline meant that the sugar plantations of the islands were likely to be chronically short of labor to work in the cane fields.

Serious attempts to supply adequate amounts of foreign labor for the plantations began with the importation of a shipload of Chinese in 1852. Planters and government officials were not always in agreement on the best sources and kinds of labor. The search for industrious and docile "coolies" went on all over the Pacific (in the hope of finding islanders racially similar to Hawaiians and satisfactory as laborers), and in most countries of Asia. A false start to immigration from Japan was made, with the importation of a single shipload of workers in 1868. Before the passage of the reciprocity treaty with the United States in 1875-1876, Chinese were the principal group of immigrant laborers.

Plantation labor, as the government and the planters soon found out, had to be replenished constantly. Its overflow into the towns, and the establishment of immigrant communities there, marked the beginning of the distinctive urban multi-racial society of modern Hawaii.

These long-term implications of the importation of plantation labor were barely noticeable when Kamehameha IV died on November 30, 1863. The new king, Kamehameha V, saw his royal task as that of being a strong ruling king as well as a reigning monarch. His most notable accomplishment was to impose upon his more or less willing native subjects, and upon the much less willing foreigners of the islands, a new constitution. The document, prepared by the king and his advisers after a stormy constitutional convention in 1864 was dissolved by royal order, vested far more power in the crown than the liberal American-influenced constitution of 1852 had done. The king's regal firmness and enterprise delighted his principal foreign adviser, Robert Crichton Wyllie, a Scot and a convinced royalist, and dismayed the Americans of Hawaii. For all that, the constitution of 1864 remained in existence for 23 years, longer than any other constitution of the Hawaiian kingdom.

Kamehameha V, like the others of his dynasty who followed Kamehameha the Great, died relatively young, in December 1872. He never married, and to complicate matters he never designated an heir, despite the entreaties of his advisers. The dynasty came to an end with him. The legislature, guided by an informal popular vote, chose as his successor the high chief William Lunalilo.

Lunalilo's reign was brief (1873-1874). He was a charming, witty man of uncertain health, unlucky enough to become king at a time of growing restlessness among his subjects. Lunalilo, like the kings before him, was faced with the necessity to come to terms with the prospect of reciprocity. He saw the economic need for it. But his people were disturbed about growing American influence in the islands. Unrest among the

Kamehameha IV (1834 - 1863)

natives spilled over in 1873 in a mutiny of the royal household troops at Honolulu. There were calls among the foreigners for protection by warships and armed foreign troops. The mutiny evaporated, the scare among the whites subsided. But Lunalilo's health was undermined by the strain, and he survived only a few months longer, dying on February 3, 1874.

Like Kamehameha V before him, Lunalilo was a bachelor who left no heir. Once again the legislature had to choose a new monarch. The two principal candidates were the high chief David Kalakaua and the dowager queen Emma, widow of Kamehameha IV. After an energetic campaign, Kalakaua was chosen in February 1874. Emma's followers rioted at Honolulu, causing a new wave of uneasiness among the whites—and an inauspicious beginning to the reign of the new king.

REVOLUTION AND COUNTERREVOLUTION

Kalakaua's relations with the white population were the central issue of his reign (1847-1891). He began by pleasing the Americans: he supported reciprocity, and his personal sponsorship of the treaty during a visit to Washington (the first visit to the capital of the United States by any reigning monarch) was at least partly responsible for the passage of the treaty.

Reciprocity was indisputably good for the islands: in 1875, on the eve of the treaty, Hawaii's export sugar crop was about 25,000,000 pounds; fifteen years later it was 250,000,000 pounds. But Kalakaua soon exhausted his credit with the whites. He was another Hawaiian king determined to rule as well as reign, and to live on a properly royal scale. He made an expensive round-the-world tour in 1882, becoming the first king to be a circumnavigator. On his return he had himself crowned in a belated and lavish coronation ceremony. He went on spending money in all sorts of ways that the taxpaying planters and merchants of the kingdom considered wasteful. There had never been so much money in Hawaii, yet under Kalakaua the national debt climbed from $388,900 in 1880 to $2,600,000 in 1890.

Kalakaua, apart from being in favor of reciprocity, was not regarded as being cordial to the white men who ran the sugar industry, and their associates, the merchants and professional men of Honolulu. He was, in fact, inclined to be antiwhite, a nativist concerned to revive Hawaiian traditions within the form of a nineteenth-century monarchy. In this he was encouraged by his principal adviser, Walter Murray Gibson, an American highly unpopular among his fellow-countrymen in Hawaii. Gibson dominated the Hawaiian cabinet from 1882 onward.

Kalakaua further alienated the established planters, a good many of whom were descended from Protestant missionary families, by encouraging a powerful economic interloper: the Californian sugar magnate Claus Spreckels. With the king's help, Spreckels was able to get favorable land leases, water rights, exclusive rights to run steamships between Hawaii and the American west coast, the right to mint coins for the kingdom, the right to lend king and country enormous sums of money at high interest—almost anything he wanted.

Gibson, meanwhile, was encouraging Kalakaua to think of Hawaii as the leading spirit in a confederation of Polynesian islands. This was a visionary conception which accomplished nothing beyond the sending of an abortive embassy to Samoa in 1885, resulting in great embarrassment for Hawaii among the real powers in the Pacific, the expansionist European nations.

By 1887, the older-established planters, merchants, lawyers and other professional and business men of Honolulu had had enough. In their view, Kalakaua's regime was ill-advised and corrupt. They, as heavy taxpayers, were being forced to finance the ruin of the islands. Led by Lorrin A. Thurston, an attorney and newspaper publisher descended from one of the first Protestant missionaries, they formed a political and military organization called the Hawaiian League, with the purpose of loosening Spreckels' grip on the economy, dislodging Gibson from the cabinet, and curbing the power of the king by a new constitution. By June 1887, they were ready for armed revolution.

The League was able to get what it wanted without bloodshed. After a mass meeting on June 30, 1887, and a show of arms, the king was

Queen Liliuokalani (1838 - 1917)

26

presented with a set of demands which had been drawn up, and to which he agreed.

The "Bayonet Constitution" of 1887 limited the king's powers very severely, and imposed a narrow franchise based on property, thus excluding perhaps three out of every four native Hawaiians from the vote. In 1887 as well, the reciprocity treaty was renewed, this time with the proviso that the United States was to have the exclusive rights to develop and use Pearl Harbor as a naval station.

Unrest grew among the natives, and in July 1889 an attempt was made to overthrow the Bayonet Constitution. A part-Hawaiian named Robert Wilcox, who as a youth had been given a military and technical education abroad at royal expense, led a night raid on Iolani Palace at Honolulu on July 30, 1889, and occupied the building with 150 men, until gunfire forced his surrender after several hours.

Beyond political opportunism, the motives of Wilcox and his followers were not clear. It was not clear, either, whether he had acted with Kalakaua's consent. The king, for whatever reason, was not at the palace when Wilcox's party occupied it. Clearly, though, Wilcox was against the white revolutionaries of 1887, the men who now controlled the government. He was tried for treason, but native jurors acquitted him.

In 1890, economic difficulties returned. The United States changed its tariff policy, doing away with duties on imported sugar and replacing them with a bounty on sugar home-grown on the American mainland. This removed altogether Hawaii's advantage under the reciprocity treaty. Sugar from the islands no longer had a protected market, and the Hawaiian industry entered on a deep depression.

This, together with a continued feeling that under a native monarchy white men in the islands would always be victims of bad government, led to a strong annexationist movement among Americans in Hawaii.

Kalakaua died on January 20, 1891 in San Francisco, during a visit to the west coast. He was succeeded by his sister Liliuokalani (1891-1893). She was the last monarch of the Hawaiian kingdom. Her ideas of royal government were stronger even than those of Kalakaua, and there was no way that they could be reconciled with the articles of the constitution of 1887.

The two years of Liliuokalani's reign were filled with heated political argument and complicated political maneuvers. In 1892, a secret

Native supporters of the monarchy rose in two ineffective rebellions against the powerful businessmen who controlled the islands.

Annexationist League was formed in Honolulu, its membership based principally on that of the Hawaiian League of 1887, and including most notably Lorrin A. Thurston and another descendant of Protestant missionaries, Sanford B. Dole.

The queen and her foreign population, led by the Americans, were clearly heading for a collision. Liliuokalani was determined to put power back into the hands of the ruling monarch; the Americans of the islands were equally determined to see that this never happened.

ANNEXATION

The collision came when on January 14, 1893, Liliuokalani dissolved the legislature in session and let it be known that she was about to proclaim a new constitution. This led the annexationists to open revolution. They took to the streets of Honolulu with arms, and by January 17 were in control of the principal government buildings. Very few shots were fired, no lives were lost. Liliuokalani surrendered her powers, and a provisional government was proclaimed. The Hawaiian monarchy was at an end.

Sanford Dole, Lorrin Thurston and the other revolutionary leaders hoped that the life of their provisional government would be short. They wanted nothing more than to see Hawaii become American soil by annexation.

One immediate problem among several was that the United States Minister to Hawaii, John L. Stevens, had been perhaps too quick to recognize the new regime. Indeed, there was a case for saying that the presence of American troops, landed at Stevens' command from a warship in the harbor, had been a crucial factor in the success of the revolution. At least, this was the view taken by the incoming Democratic administration of Grover Cleveland at Washington. After inquiries, an attempt was made by Cleveland to arrange for Liliuokalani's reinstatement.

This ran aground on the determination of the revolutionaries, who on July 4, 1894, brought into effect a republican constitution, and set about to wait until times were more favorable in Washington.

Liliuokalani's supporters, mostly native, could not wait upon events. In January 1895, a counter-revolution, led once again by Robert Wilcox, put Honolulu and its surrounding valleys under arms for a few days. It was a pathetic affair. The royalists were easily put to flight, then systematically flushed out of their refuges. Once again a series of treason trials was held, and Queen Liliuokalani herself was given a sentence of house imprisonment.

During the entire life of the Hawaiian Republic, the question of annexation was debated at Washington. The United States had always been a continental nation. The acquisition of territories in distant places was a momentous step, not to be taken lightly. Still, expansionism was in the air in the 1890s. The doctrine that it was the nation's Manifest Destiny to become an imperial power was popular, especially among Republicans.

It was during the Republican administration of William McKinley that Hawaii's destiny was decided. The case for annexing Hawaii became part of the greater question of the Spanish-American War of 1898. Spain's colonial empire included the Philippines, and in the excitement of discovering a new political and strategic role for the United States in the Pacific, the annexation of Hawaii, the key to the northern Pacific,

Sanford Ballard Dole (1844 - 1926)

became assured. By a joint resolution of Congress, successfully completed on July 7, 1898, Hawaii was annexed. The Stars and Stripes was hoisted in the islands on August 12, 1898. Sanford B. Dole, the revolutionary who became President of the Hawaiian Republic, became the first governor of the territory of Hawaii, when the new organic laws took effect in 1900.

U. S. TERRITORY

The revolution of 1893 and the annexation movement that followed are often referred to as nothing but products of the Hawaiian sugar industry. Certainly there were the closest of associations between the men who owned and administered the sugar plantations and the men who organized and carried through the revolution. And just as certainly the most substantial tie between Hawaii and the United States, of an economic kind at least, was the one brought into being and maintained by the sugar industry.

This kind of simple explanation, however, neglects other important, perhaps crucial, factors. The style of government of the Kalakaua dynasty was distasteful to Americans in the islands on grounds other than purely economic. Revolutionaries from 1887 on saw themselves more as "good government men" than as mere self-interested sugar men. And the annexationists of the 1890s regarded themselves far more strongly as American patriots, devotedly helping to work out the Manifest Destiny of their parent nation, than as men in isolation from their homeland, working out a narrow local economic interest.

Indeed, it was not the undivided opinion of white men in the islands that annexation to the United States would be good for Hawaiian sugar. To be sure, Hawaii as American soil would not have the continuous worry over American sugar tariff policy that Hawaii as a foreign country had had. But then, Hawaii as American soil would necessarily fall under American legal control, and this, in the circumstances, might very well turn out to be disadvantageous to the cost structure of the island plantation companies. To be specific, Hawaii as American soil would be subject to national controls on immigration. And at the turn of the century, opinion on the mainland was hardening discernibly against the continued admission of Oriental immigrants, the very people upon whose continued presence in great numbers the sugar industry of the islands depended absolutely for survival.

As annexation became more and more a practical possibility in the 1890s, therefore, the plantation owners hurried to bring in as many Oriental laborers as they could in advance of any prospective prohibition. Most of the workers came from Japan. After the false start in 1868, importation of Japanese laborers began in earnest in 1887, and became more and more significant thereafter. By the year 1900, when American law became definitive in Hawaii, there were more than 60,000 Japanese in the islands. In 1907 the United States, under the so-called Gentlemen's Agreement with the government of Japan, called a formal halt to the bringing in of Japanese. But even after that, more Japanese, many of them women, continued to be admitted to Hawaii, until 1924, when national immigration policy was hardened, stopping the flow almost completely. By 1920, 42.7% of the population of the Hawaiian Islands was Japanese.

Even the Japanese, readily available as they were, proved not sufficient in numbers to keep Hawaii's plantations fully staffed. Looking for a useful supplementary source, the plantation companies found one in the Philippines. In terms of immigration policy, the Philippines had the useful attribute of being under American control—they had passed from Spain to the hands of the United States as a result of the Spanish-American War of 1898. Between 1907 and the start of World War Two, more than 100,000 Filipinos, the overwhelming majority of them men, were imported as plantation laborers. Altogether the major groups of immigrants—Chinese, Japanese, Filipinos—and smaller contingents of Koreans, Portuguese, Spaniards, Russians, and other immigrants added a total of something like 400,000 to the statistics of population increase in Hawaii. By no means all of them stayed in the islands, but enough did to create a new population.

Thus, in the long run, the labor policy of the plantation companies became the population policy of the islands. In terms of economics, Hawaii was in the hands of the men who ran the sugar industry (and its associated industry, the growing and canning of pineapples, which became increasingly important in the twentieth century, emerging as a money-earner second only to sugar). Economic power was overwhelmingly centralized in the hands of five major companies, whose fortunes, founded on sugar, grew with the expanding and diversifying economy of the islands: Castle and Cooke, Alexander and Baldwin, C. Brewer, American Factors, and Theo. H. Davies. A sixth major company, the Dillingham Corporation, was not a sugar house, but matched the other five in size and influence during the

Children of Hawaii on Annexation Day, 1898.

period before World War Two. The political arrangements of the islands flowed from the economic arrangements. In general, the prevailing view of politics in Hawaii depended on the maintenance of Hawaii as one big plantation, with a hierarchy of labor organized by race and nationality, so that Orientals remained in the fields and the mills, leaving management and ownership to white men. In essence, this economic, social and political structure remained constant in Hawaii from the start of the twentieth century to World War Two. Elections were dominated by the Republican Party, the party of property. It was, in its leadership at least, a party of white men, and it had the support of the Hawaiian and part-Hawaiian population, in what amounted to an anti-Oriental alliance.

In the early decades of Hawaii's life as a territory of the United States, the maintenance of these structures presented no great problems, because, although the immigrants as a group dominated the population figures, they were aliens ineligible for citizenship, and therefore ineligible to vote in elections.

By the same token, however, the Oriental population could be seen as a force in politics in the not too distant future, because the second generation, children of immigrant parents, born in the islands, would be Americans by birth, and thus entitled to all the freedoms and responsibilities of citizenship, including the vote.

Particularly during the 1920s and 1930s, the matter of the Americanization of the Oriental emerged as a great and controversial topic of political argument and experimentation.

The situation was nothing if not complex. The first generation of Orientals, the immigrants, not unnaturally kept quite close cultural and even political ties with their homelands. To perpetuate these ties they set up churches, schools, newspapers, community associations and other institutions. Not unnaturally as well, they wanted to see their children brought up as far as possible within the old cultural traditions. And yet by law and by residence, the children were Americans as well as Orientals, members of American society as well as members of immigrant families.

The institution which provoked the greatest amount of heated argument and governmental intervention was the language school. Chinese and Japanese children educated in the public schools often went after regular school hours for a supplementary education in the language, religion and culture of their parents' homeland. The

Pearl Harbor about 1880

December 7, 1941.

most determined Americanizers in the white community of Hawaii came to believe that these schools, as long as they were allowed to continue to exist, would present insuperable obstacles to the social assimilation of the young Orientals. Eventually legislation was passed against the schools in the territorial legislature. Lawsuits followed, and the issue was fought all the way up to the United States Supreme Court, where in 1927 a judgment was handed down affirming the legality and constitutionality of the language schools. They continued to operate.

The Supreme Court judgment caused the Americanizers even more dissatisfaction. Their anxiety and concern about the immigrant population and its American offspring increased markedly during the 1930s. By this time the question had ceased to be merely a local one, limited in its implications to Hawaii. The Japanese had emerged as the biggest single group in the population of the islands at the same time as the Japanese Empire was emerging as a political and military threat to the interests of the United States in the Pacific.

By the mid-1930s, Hawaii seemed as precariously placed as it had ever been. It was the forward base of the American armed forces in the Pacific, with Pearl Harbor highly developed as the home of the Pacific Fleet and Schofield Barracks in central Oahu the biggest Army installation in the nation—and all this in a place where people of Japanese ancestry formed the biggest single identifiable portion of the population.

The question of the loyalty of Hawaii's Japanese population in the case of war was problematical. It could only be resolved by war.

PEARL HARBOR

At 7:55 a.m. on Sunday, December 7, 1941, carrier-based fighters and bombers of the Japanese Empire attacked Pearl Harbor and other military installations on Oahu, sinking a number of battleships and other heavy vessels, and inflicting in one morning the worst damage to American armed strength in the history of the nation.

Martial law was declared in the islands on Pearl Harbor day, and remained in effect until late in the war, despite the vigorous efforts of some members of the civilian administration to have it lifted after the theater of conflict in the Pacific moved further and further west, away from Hawaii, as the tide of battle turned.

To begin with, in the hours that followed the attack on Pearl Harbor, the entire Japanese population of Hawaii, about 160,000, was under suspicion of complicity, and there were tense days before it became clear that the first devastating attack was not to be followed by invasion.

Among the Japanese community, a number of Buddhist and Shinto priests, language teachers, newspaper editors, and other leading figures were arrested and interned, first in Hawaii, then on the mainland—in all, less than one percent of the Japanese of Hawaii. Investigations during and after the war by the FBI and other agencies confirmed that no Hawaii Japanese was guilty of espionage or sabotage.

For the younger Japanese, those born in the islands, the great test of loyalty was to fight under the American flag. Those who wanted the opportunity were at first denied it. The armed forces would not take them as recruits. After a year of war the Army reconsidered, and an all-Japanese volunteer unit was formed. First as the 100th Battalion, then as the 442nd Regimental Combat Team, the young Japanese, *nisei* in their parents' language, Americans of Japanese ancestry by their own designation, fought with great distinction in the European theater. They became the most highly decorated unit in the United States armed forces.

The war changed Hawaiian society irreversibly. There was no chance that after 1945 things would revert to their pre-war condition. The most easily visible sign was that the Oriental population became politically active and influential. This movement was led to a large extent by war veterans, including many members of the 442nd, who went on to college after the war on the GI Bill, and then took a law degree and went into politics. Given the domination of the islands by the Republican Party in the great days of the plantation society, it was predictable that the new generation of Oriental politicians and voters would attach themselves for the most part to the Democratic Party. After the first few years of organization in the post-war period, the Democratic Party established itself as a genuinely multi-racial organization, broadly based on the diverse population of the islands. This became in turn its guarantee of success at the polls. By 1954, with Republicans in power nationally, the Democrats became the party of power in Hawaii. They were able to remain in power all through the rest of the 1950s and all through the 1960s.

Contemporary with the rise of the Democratic Party, and connected with it in many ways, was the rise of an organized labor movement in the islands. This again was part of a great social transformation. As early as the beginning of the twentieth century, there had been strikes on the plantations from time to time, some of them long and bitter, involving thousands of workers. To handle the labor problem, the plantation companies used a mixture of methods, ranging from the introduction of strike-breaking workers to sensible and humane concessions strategically timed. Compared with the situation on the American mainland, the life of an agricultural laborer on a Hawaiian plantation was by no means bad, and it compared favorably even with the life of a good many mainland industrial workers. This comparison, of course, was not one made by the workers themselves, and when it was brought to their attention it did not make them any the less interested in labor organizations which might bring further improvements.

If the labor movement was not quick to grow to a position of strength, this was due principally to the mixed racial and national origins of the work force of the plantations. Communication and cooperation were difficult between native Hawaiians and part-Hawaiians, Chinese, Japanese and Filipinos. All the plantation strikes before World War Two were mounted by workers organized according to nationality, and this meant that there was no industry-wide workers' program of any significance.

The modern labor movement got definitively under way with the passage by Congress in 1935 of the National Labor Relations Act and the affirmation of its constitutionality by a decision of the Supreme Court in 1937. This opened the way for systematic organization of unions in Hawaii as elsewhere in the nation. A good deal depended, in the case of the mechanized plantations of Hawaii, on having workers classified for organizational purposes as industrial rather than agricultural, because the national legislation was aimed at factory rather than farm. Decisions of the National Labor Relations Board favored industrial classification for the great bulk of Hawaii's plantation workers, and with this established, organization could go ahead with every prospect of substantial success.

The first successful union organizers were men who had had experience in the maritime unions of the American west coast, and in fact organization in Hawaii was begun on the waterfront, spreading from there to the plantations. The International Longshoremen's and Warehousemen's Union emerged as the chief spokesman of the workers, and had just succeeded in writing the first sizeable contracts with management when World War Two broke out.

Labor organization was effectively brought to a halt during the war under martial law, with its restrictions on civil liberty and industrial mobility. But after peace returned, the same forces which brought the Democratic Party to a position of strength at the polls created a labor movement which could number its members in the tens of thousands. The ILWU went into politics vigorously, and during the early years of its post-

Lei Lady

war activities, it sometimes seemed on the brink of taking over the Democratic Party altogether. This never happened, but then and later endorsement by organized labor was regarded as a considerable asset to a political candidate.

In the course of establishing its dominant position in the post-war years, the ILWU, under its leader Jack Hall, called several major strikes on the plantations, and an extremely long and bitter one on the waterfront in 1949. As virtually all of Hawaii's commerce was seaborne, this was tantamount to bringing the economy to a standstill—evidence of the tremendous power organized labor had come to wield.

The tactics of the ILWU were undoubtedly extreme, too much so for a good many Democratic politicians, certainly so for almost all Republicans. Some of the union leaders came out

but with the passing of the years it became less and less so. By the 1950s Hawaii's population was larger than that of several states at the time of their admission. Its tax payments to the federal treasury were likewise larger than those of several states. It had been a territory for longer than any other before admission. Under the law of the territory, framed by Congress, the voters of Hawaii did not elect their own governor, and their most important judges were presidential appointees. Their single elected representative in Congress had a voice but no vote. Congress could still alter at will the sugar legislation crucial to Hawaii, and had indeed done so for a short time in the 1930s. Congress in fact could alter the form of government of the islands, and this had taken place when martial law was imposed after the attack on Pearl Harbor.

On August 21, 1959 Hawaii was admitted to the Union as the Fiftieth State.

of the Marxist-oriented maritime unions of the 1930s. These facts, considered in the general climate of the Cold War of the early 1950s, led to several investigations of Communism in Hawaii by Congressional committees. The upshot was that in 1953 Jack Hall and six others, among them some Orientals, were tried and convicted under the Smith Act (their convictions were eventually reversed on appeal).

STATEHOOD CELEBRATION

The question of Communism became a stumbling block to the realization of the great ambition of the people of the islands: to see Hawaii admitted to the union of states. Since Hawaii became a territory in 1900, there had been periodical review of its status. The political arrangement had been satisfactory enough to begin with,

Once again, it was the experience of World War Two that got a sustained statehood movement under way. The feeling of a majority of people in the islands was that the war record of the people of Hawaii, from Pearl Harbor to V-J Day, was that of people who deserved to be regarded as first-class citizens. Their loyalty to the United States could not sensibly be regarded as deficient. Statehood should be theirs, as a matter of justice, as a matter of right.

In fact, the first congressional hearings on the subject of statehood for Hawaii were held as early as 1935, but it was not until 1959 that the matter was finally resolved.

The idea of statehood for Hawaii took a long time to gain authority in Washington. Hearings multiplied, legislation was framed and discussed but never passed. In a sense, the arguments over statehood were not much more than a repetition of the debate over the annexation of Hawaii in

1898. To some congressmen, and particularly to some Southern senators, the fact that Hawaii was distant from the mainland, and that its population was mixed and getting more so with each generation, seemed to argue against admitting the islands as a state on the basis of equality with other states. Newer issues were added to this old one. The power of the labor unions was deplored. It was alleged that Communists dominated the government and society of the territory. Such assertions, rebuttals, claims and counterclaims about the real nature of society in Hawaii kept the issue alive throughout the 1950s.

Not until 1959 did Congressional Delegate John Burns and the other leaders of the statehood movement taste success. On several earlier occasions, Congress had arrived at the point of giving serious consideration to a statehood bill, but it had never been possible to maneuver a bill through both houses. Now the best opportunity of all arose. Alaska was being considered for statehood at the same time, and a strategy of permitting Alaska to become the 49th state was developed. Once this was accomplished, the logic and reasonability of admitting Hawaii were clear to all who mattered, and passage of the necessary legislation was assured. On March 11, 1959 the Senate passed a statehood bill; the House followed suit on March 12; a plebiscite in Hawaii produced a majority in favor of admission of 17 to 1; and on Admission Day, August 21, 1959, Hawaii became the 50th state.

Like reciprocity and annexation before it, this new attachment to the nation brought with it an economic boom. In the decade that followed statehood, Hawaii became populous and prosperous as never before. The economic base changed: sugar and pineapple were supplemented and finally supplanted as prime money earners by tourism and federal spending, the bulk of the latter military in application. The jet plane, which was the making of the tourist industry, encouraged closer connections between Hawaii and the mainland, and this in turn influenced a new kind of migration to Hawaii: mainland Americans, who by the end of the 1960s were arriving in such numbers to take up residence that a future was foreseeable in which a situation new to Hawaii in the twentieth century would develop—one ethnic group would comprise an absolute majority of the population. Increasingly, the style of life of the islands was assimilated to that of the mainland. The passage from undiscovered islands to statehood had taken less than two hundred years.

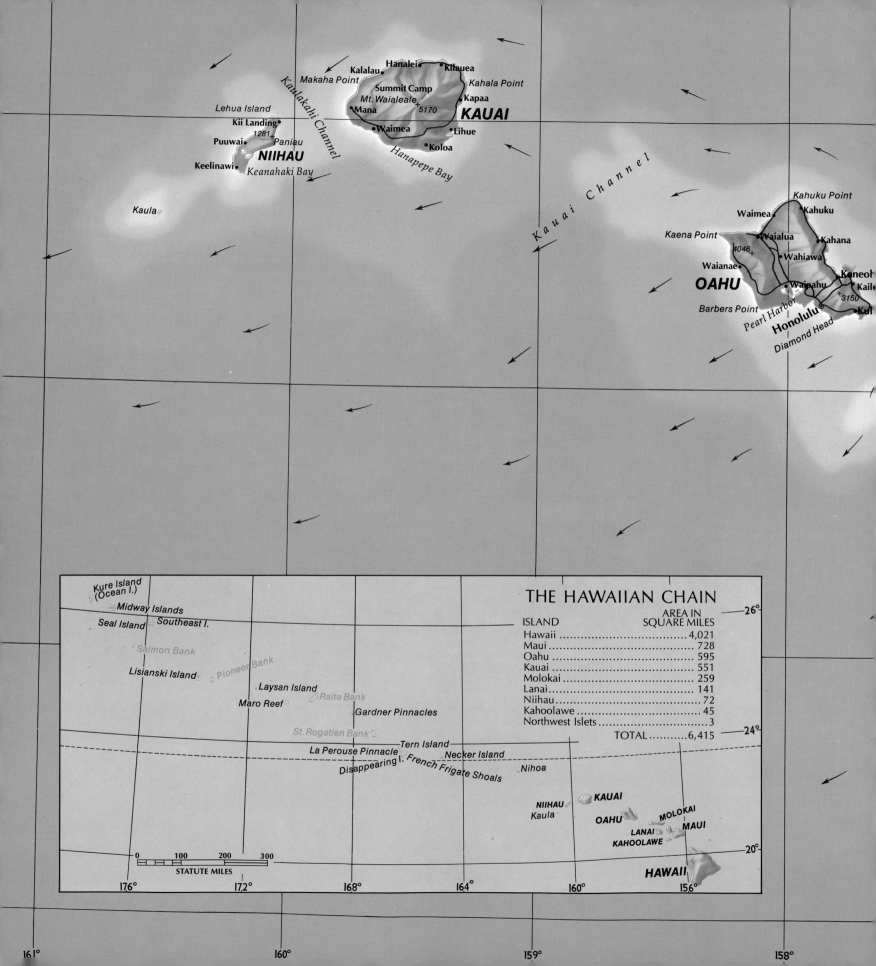

Kalalau
Hanalei
Kilauea
Makaha Point
Kahala Point
Summit Camp
Mt. Waialeale
Kapaa
Lehua Island
+5170
KAUAI
Kii Landing
Mana
1281+
Paniau
Waimea
Lihue
Puuwai
Koloa
Keelinawi
NIIHAU
Kaulakahi Channel
Keanahaki Bay
Hanapepe Bay

Kaula

Kauai Channel

Kahuku Point
Waimea
Kahuku
Kaena Point
Waialua
Kahana
4046+
Wahiawa
Waianae
Kaneoh
OAHU
Waipahu
Kail
+3150
Barbers Point
Pearl Harbor
Honolulu
Ku
Diamond Head

Kure Island
(Ocean I.)
Midway Islands
Seal Island
Southeast I.
Salmon Bank
Pioneer Bank
Lisianski Island
Laysan Island
Raita Bank
Maro Reef
Gardner Pinnacles
St. Rogatien Bank
Tern Island
La Perouse Pinnacle
Necker Island
Disappearing I. *French Frigate Shoals*
Nihoa

THE HAWAIIAN CHAIN

ISLAND	AREA IN SQUARE MILES
Hawaii	4,021
Maui	728
Oahu	595
Kauai	551
Molokai	259
Lanai	141
Niihau	72
Kahoolawe	45
Northwest Islets	3
TOTAL	6,415

NIIHAU
KAUAI
Kaula
OAHU
MOLOKAI
LANAI
MAUI
KAHOOLAWE

HAWAII

0 100 200 300
STATUTE MILES

26°
24°
20°

176° 172° 168° 164° 160° 156°

161° 160° 159° 158°

The Principal
HAWAIIAN ISLANDS

0   25   50
STATUTE MILES

MAP SYMBOLS

—— Roads
═══ Dual Lane Roads
---- Trails
(69) Highway Numbers
(HI) Interstate

✈ Commercial Airfields
✈ Military Airfields
Coral Reef
Swamp
← Warm Currents
Elevations in Feet

Special Points of Interest
□ Other Points of Interest
Heiau (Ancient Temple)
Petroglyphs (Rock Paintings)
∴ Ruins

MOLOKAI
Ilio Point
Moomomi
epuhi
una Loa +1381 Kalaupapa
Hoolehua Halawa
Kaunakakai 4970+ Pukoo
Kamalo

Pailolo Channel

MAUI
Pohakuloa Pt.
Kaena Point
Kaanapali Honokohau
Lahaina 5788+ Wailuku Pauwela
Kahului Kailua
Olowalu
Honomaele
Waiakoa Red Hill Hana
Kamaole 10023 Koali
Nuu
Keoneoio

LANAI
+1799
Lanai City +3370
Kaumalapau
Palaoa Point
Manele Bay
Kukui Point

KAHOOLAWE
+1477

Alenuihaha Channel

HAWAII
Upolu Point
Hawi Kohala
Mahukona
Waipio Kukuihaele
Honokaa
Kawaihae 5505+ Paauilo
Waimea Laupahoehoe
(Kamuela) Hakalau
Kiholo
Mauna Kea Papaikou
Puuanahulu 13796
Mahaiula Hilo
Pohakuloa
Keaau (Olaa)
Kailua
Kainaliu Mountain View
Kealakekua Pahoa
Mauna Loa Pohoiki
Honaunau +13680
4077 Kilauea Crater
Koa Mill Kalapana
Miloli Pahala
Ninole
Waiohinu Naalehu

Ka Lae (South Point)

22°
21°
20°
19°

157° 156° 155° 154°

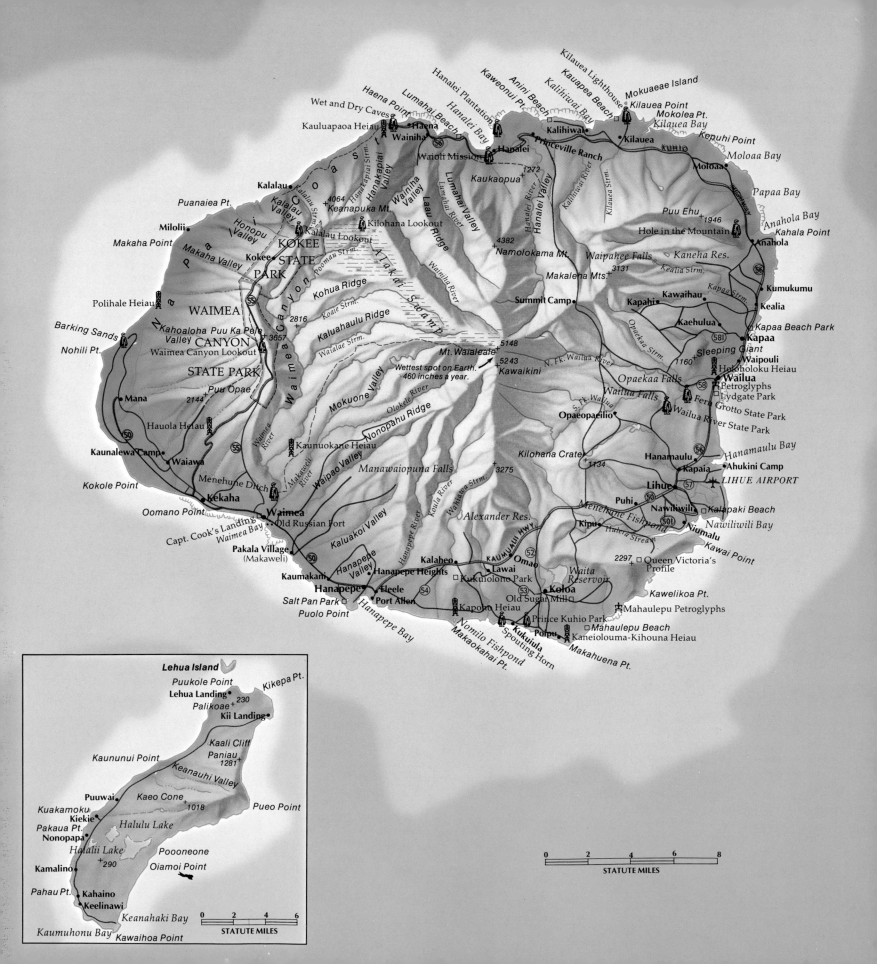

Kauai and Niihau

Kauai, the people of old believed, is the eldest of the twelve children born to Wakea, the Sky God, and Papa, the Earth Mother. Despite her age, Kauai is "beautiful beyond compare." Romantic newcomers in the Nineteenth Century called Kauai "The Garden Isle." A single volcano made this island: Waialeale's high, curved rampart is the eastern rim of the huge caldera, the largest in the Hawaiian Chain. Erosion has filled the caldera almost to its brim and has carved deep valleys in its flanks.

Niihau, purchased from King Kamehameha V in 1864 by Mrs. Elizabeth Sinclair, is owned by her descendants, the Robinson family of Kauai. Niihau's 266 residents, almost all of whom are Hawaiians or part-Hawaiians, maintain the Robinsons' cattle ranch.

1

LIHUE is the capital of Kauai County (which includes Niihau). In 1978 the income of Kauai's 34,700 residents came from tourists and five sugar plantations.

2

WAIMEA CANYON, a miniature Grand Canyon of the Colorado, is 10 miles long, 2,857 feet deep at its highest point.

3

WAIMEA   Captain James Cook and members of his exploring expedition, who discovered these islands on January 18, 1778, made their first landing at Waimea two days later.

4

MENEHUNE DITCH   About a mile inland, on Waimea River's western bank, a short section of the menehune ditch still helps to irrigate the villagers' taro patches.

5

FORT ELIZABETH   Just east of Waimea, at the river's mouth, lie the ruins of Fort Elizabeth, a trading post and fortress built by Russians in 1815-1816.

6

MOUNT WAIALEALE, 5,240 feet high, is considered to be the world's "rainiest spot." Average annual rainfall is 486 inches; in fiscal year 1947-1948 rain gauges measured 624.1 inches.

7

KOLOA   Hawaii's first successful sugar plantation was started at Koloa in 1835.

8

HAUPU RIDGE   German immigrants explained the name of east Kauai's seaport by pointing to Haupu Ridge. There, in basalt sculptured by wind and rain, matronly Queen Victoria lifts a reproving finger at naughty nephew Kaiser Wilhelm. She is saying, of course, "Na, Wili, Wili."

9

WAILUA VALLEY   The ruins of many ancient temples can be found in Wailua Valley, once the residence of Kauai's kings. Best preserved are Holoholoku heiau and the royal birthstones.

10

NAPALI COAST   You can see some of these spectacular cliffs if you'll walk about a hundred yards along the trail which begins at Haena.

11

KALALAU VALLEY   Don't miss the view of Kalalau Valley from the lookout near Kokee, 4,000 feet above the distant sea.

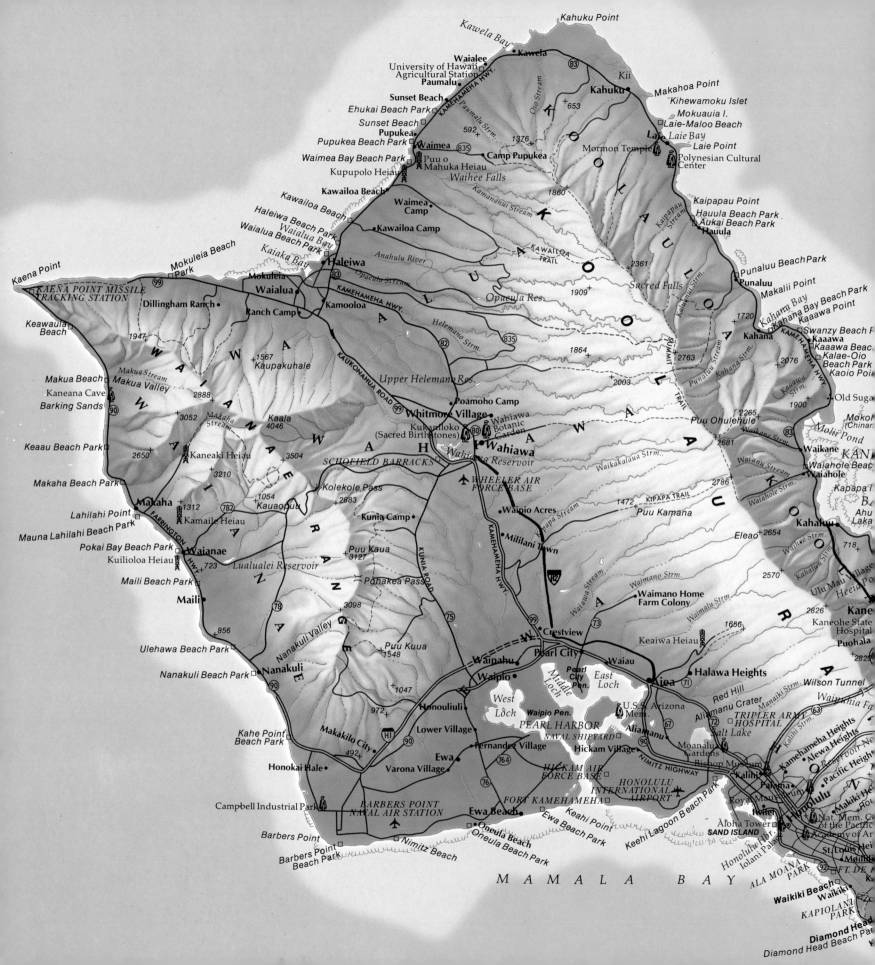

Oahu

Oahu means "The Gathering Place." The little port on its southern shore, the only protected harbor in all Hawaii, drew foreigners and their ships to Honolulu, making it the Crossroads of the Pacific and the major portal of entry for people and their possessions coming to these islands.

This island is about 40 miles long and 26 wide, and has an area of 595 square miles. In 1978, its 719-543 people managed to drive almost 435,000 motor vehicles. Major sources of income are tourists, military establishments, agencies of federal, state, and county governments, four sugar plantations, three pineapple companies, and the innumerable service industries concerned in maintaining the state's residents and visitors.

1

WAIANAE MOUNTAINS in the west and the Koolau Mountains in the east are the remnants of the two great volcanoes which made Oahu.

2

IOLANI PALACE, a symbol of old Hawaii, was restored in 1978. Built for King Kalakaua in 1879–1881, and used after the monarchy as an office building, it is now a museum open to the public.

3

BERNICE P. BISHOP MUSEUM, founded in 1889, is the primary repository for relics of Hawaii's past. Its research programs are concerned with Polynesia's past, present, and future.

4

PUNCHBOWL In the crater of Punchbowl, once called Puu-o-waina, Hill of Sacrifice, the remains of American soldiers, sailors, and marines lie in the National Memorial Cemetery of the Pacific.

5

SEA LIFE PARK, near Makapuu Point, exhibits living creatures from the sea. At adjacent Oceanic Institute, marine biologists study them.

6

USS ARIZONA MEMORIAL The United States Navy offers an instructive tour of the USS Arizona Memorial, dedicated to victims of Japan's attack upon Pearl Harbor on December 7, 1941.

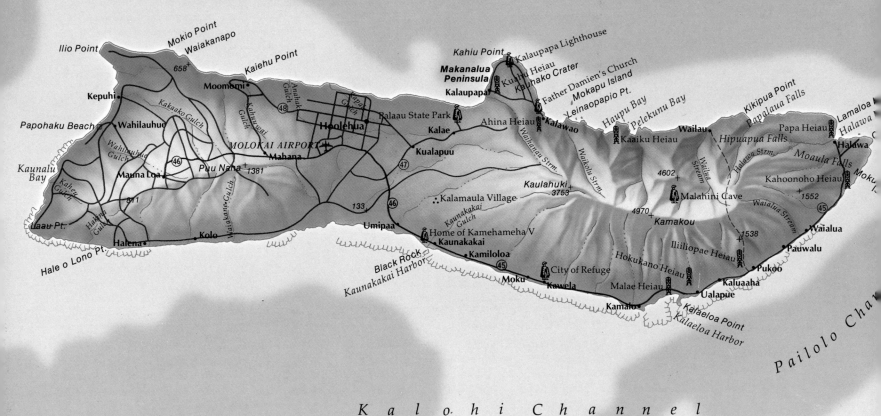

Molokai

Ilio Point
Mokio Point
Waiakanapo
Kaiehu Point
658
Moomomi
Kepuhi
Kahiu Point
Kalaupapa Lighthouse
Makanalua Peninsula
Kuahu Heiau
Kauhako Crater
Kalaupapa
Father Damien's Church
Mokapu Island
Yeinaopapio Pt.
Palaau State Park
Kakaako Gulch
Kaluwai Gulch
Napa Gulch
Anahaki Gulch
Papohaku Beach
Wahilauhue
Hoolehua
Kalae
Ahina Heiau
Kalawao
Haupu Bay
Pelekunu Bay
Wailau
Kikipua Point
Papalaua Falls
Lamaloa
Halawa
Papa Heiau
MOLOKAI AIRPORT
Mahana
48
Kualapuu
Kaaiku Heiau
Hipuapua Falls
Moaula Falls
Kaunalu Bay
Wahilauhue Gulch
46
Puu Nana
1381
Kahili Gulch
47
Waikolu Strm.
Wailau Stream
Halawa Strm.
Waialua Stream
Kahoonoho Heiau
1552
Mauna Loa
811
Waiakane Gulch
Kaulahuki
3753
4602
1538
45
Laau Pt.
Hanne Gulch
133
46
Kalamaula Village
Kaunakakai Gulch
Malahini Cave
4970
Kamakou
Iliiliopae Heiau
Waialua
Halena
Kolo
Umipaa
Home of Kamehameha V
Kaunakakai
Hokukano Heiau
Pauwalu
Hale o Lono Pt.
Black Rock
Kaunakakai Harbor
Kamiloloa
45
City of Refuge
Moku
Kawela
Malae Heiau
Pukoo
Kaluaaha
Ualapue
Kamalo
Kalaeloa Point
Kalaeloa Harbor

Kalohi Channel

Pailolo Channel

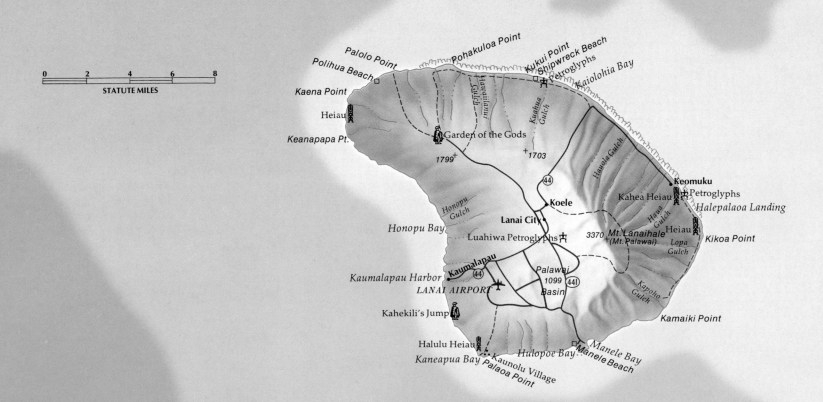

Lanai

Palolo Point
Pohakuloa Point
Kukui Point
Shipwreck Beach
Petroglyphs
Polihua Beach
Kaiolohia Bay
Kaena Point
Heiau
Hawaiilanui Gulch
Kuahua Gulch
Keanapapa Pt.
Garden of the Gods
1799
1703
Haola Gulch
Keomuku
Kahea Heiau
Petroglyphs
44
Koele
Halepalaoa Landing
Honopu Gulch
Haa Gulch
Honopu Bay
Lanai City
Luahiwa Petroglyphs
Heiau
Kikoa Point
3370 Mt. Lanaihale
(Mt. Palawai)
Lopa Gulch
Kaumalapau
44
Palawai
441
Kapoho Gulch
Kaumalapau Harbor
LANAI AIRPORT
1099 Basin
Kamaiki Point
Kahekili's Jump
Halulu Heiau
Hulopoe Bay
Manele Bay
Kaneapua Bay
Kaunolu Village
Manele Beach
Palaoa Point

0   2   4   6   8
STATUTE MILES

Molokai and Lanai

Long ago, Molokai, Lanai, and Maui were united in a single island. Since 1905 they have been joined politically, to constitute Maui County.

After the long body of Molokai had been produced by two major volcanoes, a little afterthought crater, midway in the northern escarpment, added the minuscule promontory of Kalaupapa. Upon this leaf of land, a settlement for Hawaii's lepers has been maintained since 1866. Isolated politically as well as physically, their promontory is Kalawao County.

About 6,400 people live on Molokai. "The Friendly Island," working for one pineapple plantation, several cattle ranches, or on their own homestead-farms.

In 1922 Dole Corporation's founder bought most of Lanai, "The Pineapple Island," from Maui's Baldwin family, for $1,100,000.

1

PHALLIC ROCK Proper maps do not show it, so ask a friendly islander where to find the most unabashed phallic rock in the United States.

2

FISHPONDS Along Molokai's southern coast are some of the few surviving stone-walled fishponds built by aboriginal Hawaiians. Marine biologists are using these in experiments to increase yields of foods from the sea.

3

AT KALAWAO, Father Damien de Veuster ministered to afflicted patients from 1873 until, a leper himself, he died in 1889. The two conjoined churches of St. Philomena and an empty grave are his memorials. His body was returned to Louvain, Belgium, in 1936.

4

SILOAMA Between Kalawao and the present Leprosarium at Kalaupapa is Siloama, the Church of the Healing Spring, a bit of Protestant New England transplanted to the tropics.

5

AXIS DEER, thriving in Molokai's wilderness, are fair game for hunters during prescribed periods. Islanders express divided opinions about the merits of releasing these deer upon the Big Island.

6

PINEAPPLES About 15,000 of Lanai's 90,200 acres are planted in pineapples.

7

KAUMALAPAU From Lanai's pocket harbor of Kaumalapau, harvested pineapples are shipped by barge to Dole Corporation's cannery in Honolulu, 60 nautical miles away.

8

PETROGLYPHS and rock platforms on which natives built their grass huts identify the ruins of several ancient villages on Lanai's windward coast.

9

NORFOLK ISLAND PINES planted as windbreaks in and around Lanai City also help to collect water from mist.

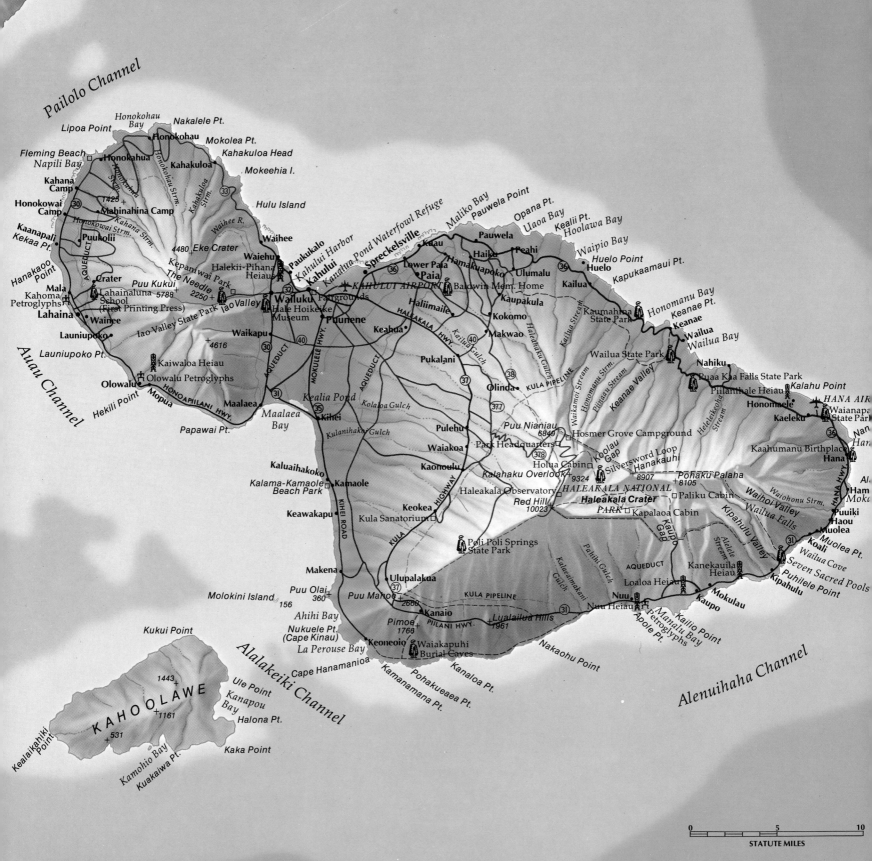

Maui and Kahoolawe

"Maui no ka oi, Maui is the best," proclaim her people, proud of their serene land, upon which the sun shines with special favor since he was slowed in his course by the folk-hero for whom the island is named. Second to Hawaii in size, Maui was formed by two volcanoes: Puu Kukui, sundered by eruptions and erosion into the spectacular gorges which give "The Valley Isle" its nickname; and Haleakala, 10,023 feet high, which encloses the world's largest dormant caldera, 21 miles in circumference. Tourists, two sugar plantations, two pineapple companies, and cattle ranches sustain Maui's 52,000 residents.

Only wild goats and sheep live now on Kahoolawe, used as a bombing target by America's armed forces since 1942.

1

LAHAINA was an important rest-and-recreation place for whalers from 1820 to 1860.

2

LAHAINALUNA SCHOOL, oldest American school west of the Rocky Mountains, was founded in 1831.

3

LAHAINA, KAANAPALI & PACIFIC RAIL-ROAD lures islanders, eager to enjoy the five-mile ride aboard the state's only passenger train.

4

LA PEROUSE BAY commemorates the five-hour visit of that ill-fated commander and his expedition on May 29, 1786. Those French explorers were the first foreigners to set foot on Maui.

5

WAILUKU is the capital of Maui County (which includes Molokai and Lanai).

6

IAO NEEDLE Near the heart of Puu Kukui's shattered crater, approached from Wailuku through narrow Iao Valley, rises Iao Needle, 2,250 feet high.

7

HAMAKUA DITCH Two great irrigation systems bring water from Haleakala's rainy northern slopes to dry Paia and Puunene. The first system, Hamakua Ditch, 17 miles long, constructed in 1876-1877 at a cost of $80,000 by Henry P. Baldwin and Samuel T. Alexander, showed island sugar planters how science could tame nature to serve their needs.

8

HALEAKALA At the top of Haleakala, House of the Sun, where Maui-of-the-Thousand-Tricks snared the impatient god, men and instruments in "Science City" now study the sun and track the courses of machines sent from earth into space.

9

SILVERSWORD The rare silversword, *Argyroxiphium sandwicensis*, grows near Haleakala's summit and in its crater.

10

MAKAWAO RODEO, held on or about July 4, presents island cowboys (of varied ancestry, hue, and size) in the usual Wild West events (complete with parade) in an idyllic Hawaiian setting.

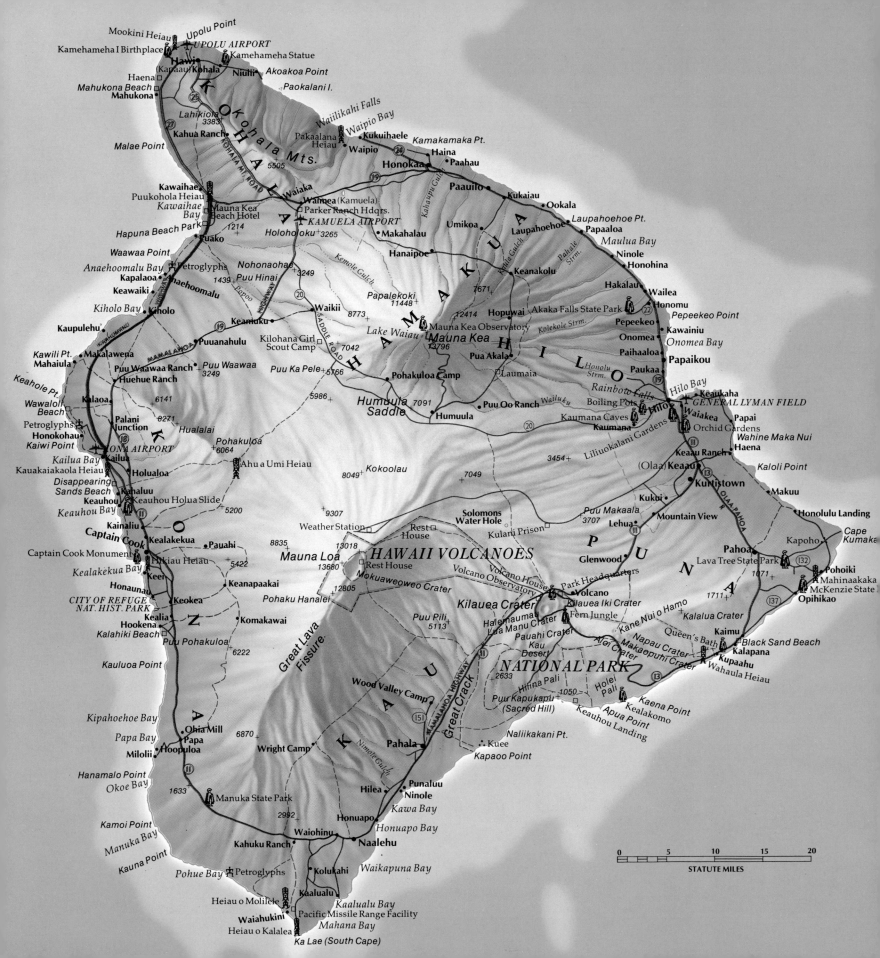

Hawaii

"The Big Island," with 4,025 square miles, has been formed by lava flows issuing from five volcanic rift-zones. The oldest, in Kohala, is inactive; Hualalai, which last erupted in 1801, and Mauna Kea probably are dormant; Mauna Loa and Kilauea, still very much awake, are the most active volcanoes on earth. For this reason, the red ohia lehua blossom, sacred to the fire-goddess Pele, is this island's official flower.

In 1978 about 81,000 people lived on Hawaii. Its economy is based upon five sugar plantations; numerous cattle ranches; vegetable farms and nurseries for orchids; tropical flowers, and foliage; orchards for coffee, macadamia nuts, and fruits; lumbering; and services for tourists.

1
KALAHIKIOLA CHURCH In peaceful Kohala look for unspoiled Pololu Valley and, unexpected evidence of New England, Kalahikiola Church, built in 1855.

2
MAUNA KEA Upon Mauna Kea's highest peaks, above clouds and dust, astronomers study the stars through telescopes in four observatories.

3
HULIHEE PALACE In Kailua are Hulihee Palace, constructed for High Chief Kuakini in 1837-1838, and Mokuaikaua Church, begun in 1836.

4
PARKER RANCH, more than 300,000 acres in extent, is about three-fourths the size of Oahu.

5
KEALAKEKUA BAY Captain James Cook, discoverer of the Hawaiian Islands, and four of his marines were killed in an affray at Kealakekua Bay on February 14, 1779.

6
THE CITY OF REFUGE at Honaunau, handsomely restored by the U.S. National Park Service in 1967-1969, shows how effectively the ancient Hawaiians used their island's resources of stone and wood.

7
KAIMU BEACH Lava rather than coral forms the black sand of Kaimu Beach near Kalapana.

8
MAUNA KEA BEACH HOTEL Near Kawaihae, elegant Mauna Kea Beach Hotel stands in contrast to the grim heathen temple of Puu Kohola, largest heiau in the islands.

9
HAWAII VOLCANOES NATIONAL PARK, created by Congress in 1916, is the abode of the fire-goddess Pele. The Park includes Mokuaweoweo, Mauna Loa's summit caldera, as well as the chain of craters which identifies the Kilauea rift zone.

10
HILO is Hawaii County's capital, major port, and site of the University of Hawaii's second campus.

11
WAIPIO VALLEY, once the home of Kohala's warring chiefs and numerous vassals, is quieter now, peopled by a handful of taro farmers.

Trees

Hawaii's flora is as cosmopolitan as are her people: somewhere in the islands, between seashore and mountain tops, a place has been found for adopted plants imported from many alien parts of the world. This diversity is most evident in the trees and flowering shrubs: cryptomerias from Japan grow among eucalypts from Australia, and frangipani from Central America bloom at the feet of towering Norfolk Island pines.

Aboriginal Hawaiians started the transformation of these new-found islands when they brought the ancestral coconuts, *kukuis,* breadfruits, mountain apples, and bananas, as well as many other food plants and medicinal herbs, from central Polynesia. In 1792, Captain George Vancouver and Dr. Archibald Menzies, his surgeon-naturalist, inaugurated the age of modern introductions when they presented Kona's chiefs with several hundred young orange plants grown from seeds obtained at the Cape of Good Hope. During the Nineteenth Century thoughtful sea captains and residents brought in dozens of new species of trees. Since 1900, government agencies and the Hawaiian Sugar Planters' Association Experiment Station have been responsible for establishing trees suitable as windbreaks or in forestation projects, and commercial nurseries have specialized in flowering ornamentals.

POINCIANA, flamboyant, *Delonix regia;* from Madagascar. Relatively small trees, with buttressing roots, twisted trunk, gnarled, irregular branches. In spring, masses of scarlet flowers touched with orange and gold burst out from every branch tip, seeming to set the tree ablaze.

MAMANE, *Sophora chrysophylla;* endemic. Leguminous shrubs to trees; prefer high elevations; clusters of pale yellow flowers at branch tips and leaf axils; winged pods bear 4 to 8 oval yellow seeds. Hawaiians used the exceedingly hard wood for sled-runners, digging sticks, and posts.

COCONUT PALM, *Cocos nucifera;* from Indo-Pacific region, "the best known palm in the world." Imported by colonizing Hawaiians as one of their essential plants, it provided food, drink, shelter, wood, cordage, ornaments, medicine, and cosmetics.

48

KIAWE, mesquite, *Prosopis pallida;* from Peru. Shrubs to large trees. Feathery mimosa-like leaves: long, sharp thorns on young branches; pale yellow florets in cylindrical spikes, long, stiff yellow pods. It enriches soil; yields nectar for honey, beans for cattle fodder, wood for charcoal.

KUKUI, candlenut, *Aleurites moluccana;* from southern Asia. Erect, tall trees; large, yellow-green to green maple-like leaves; clusters of small white flowers; fleshy green fruits enclosing one or two black nuts. Hawaiians burned nutmeats (or their oil) for light, made ornaments from polished shells.

MONKEYPOD, *Samanea saman;* from Central America. Large spreading trees, forming great domes of dark green leaves; feathery pink puffs of flowers appear in spring, followed by long, dark, wrinkled pods. Bowls, trays, furniture are made from the beautifully grained wood.

GOLDEN SHOWER, Indian laburnum, *Cassia fistula;* from India. Tall trees, with dark green compound leaves composed of 4 to 8 pairs of broad, pointed leaflets; large, drooping clusters of brilliant yellow flowers; straight, dark brown, cylindrical seed pods 1 to 2 feet long.

TRAVELLERS' TREE, *Ravenala madagascarensis;* from Madagascar. This strange thing resembles a flattened banana plant grafted upon a palm stump, bearing gigantic white birds-of-paradise for flowers. Rainwater collected at the base of each leaf can be tapped by thirsty travellers.

INDIAN BANYAN, *Ficus benghalensis;* from India. Enormous spreading trees, with thick central trunks, huge arching branches supported by stiltlike secondary trunks formed by swelling of aerial rootlets. Canopy of dark green ovate leaves, with pairs of small, round, cherry-red fruits.

Native Birds

Only a few kinds of land birds accidentally found their way across the more than 2,000 miles of ocean that separate the Hawaiian Islands from North America and Asia. About 15 ancestral species from 11 families of birds did reach the islands in the distant past. In the absence of competition and predators these ancestors evolved to form about 70 different kinds of birds that are unique to the Hawaiian Islands. In addition to such birds as a goose, two kinds of ducks, and a hawk, one entire family is found only in the Hawaiian Islands. This is the Hawaiian honeycreeper family (Drepanididae). The honeycreepers illustrate the process of organic evolution on isolated oceanic islands to a finer degree than any other bird family in the world. Unfortunately, about 40 percent of these unique Hawaiian birds already are extinct. Another third are rare and endangered. This is a tragic situation because when a species of plant or animal becomes extinct, it is lost forever.

'APAPANE right

The 'Apapane, Himatione sanguinea, is the most common of the surviving species of honeycreepers, and is found on all the main Hawaiian Islands. Gregarious during much of the year and vociferous in the nesting season, the 'apapane frequents the tops of forest trees. When it feeds on the bright red flowers of the 'ohi'a lehua, the 'apapane may be hard to see, even though its body feathers are deep crimson.

'I'IWI far right

Few birds are as striking as the brilliant orange-red 'I'iwi, Vestiaria coccinea, with its black wings and tail and long, curved, salmon-colored bill. The birds feed on insects and a variety of flowers, including the endemic lobelias. Abundant on all main islands in the 1890s, now the 'i'iwi is common only on Kauai, Maui, and Hawaii.

'ELEPAIO *below left*

The 'Elepaio, *Chasiempis sandwichensis,* is an Old World flycatcher that inhabits the forests of Kauai, Oahu, and Hawaii. Less than six inches in total length, the *'elepaio* is an inquisitive bird, often hopping from branch to branch close to a person standing still in the jungle. Perhaps because of one of its primary songs, " *'e-le-pa-i-o,"* this bird was important in Hawaiian folklore.

'IO *right*

The *'Io* or Hawaiian Hawk, *Buteo solitarius,* is one of the endangered species. It is a diurnal bird of prey that lives primarily on mice, rats, spiders, and insects. The females, about 18 inches in length, are larger than the males. These broad-winged, soaring birds are found only on the island of Hawaii.

53

MAMO *below right*

The Black *Mamo* or *'O'o-nuku-mu, Drepanis funerea,* a honeycreeper, subsisted almost entirely on nectar, and was especially partial to the tubular flowers of several species of lobelias. The birds often fed only a foot or so from the ground. As a bird inserted its bill deeply into a flower, the sticky, whitish pollen adhered to the feathers on the top of the bird's head, and thus was carried to other flowers. The birds usually were tame, not infrequently following a person through the forest, and responding to imitations of their calls. The Black *Mamo* was discovered on Molokai by R. C. L. Perkins in 1893. The birds were not common, and the last specimens were collected about 1907. No one has seen a *mamo* since that time.

'O'O *far right*

Once termed the "prince, or king, of Hawaiian plumage-birds," the Hawaii 'O'o, *Moho nobilis,* a honey eater, was first collected during the visit of Captain Cook's expedition in 1779. The birds were more than a foot in length, and their yellow feathers were highly valued by Hawaiians for making feather capes and headdresses. It has been estimated that the yellow feathers from nearly 80,000 'o'o and *mamo, Drepanis pacifica,* were used to make the splendid feather cloak of Kamehameha the Great. Although considered a common bird in the early 1890s, the last of the magnificent 'o'o apparently were killed soon after the turn of the century. Only the Kauai 'O'o, which has fewer yellow feathers than any of the other species, is still to be found in the Alakai Swamp, but in such small numbers that its survival remains uncertain.

Illustrations from Walter Rothschild. 1893-1900. "The Avifauna of Laysan and the Hawaiian Possessions," and S. B. Wilson and A. H. Evans. 1890-1899. "Aves Hawaiienses."

Native Plants

The native flora, once upon a time, consisted of about 1800 species, 96 percent of which grew no where else in the world. Many of these endemic plants have been exterminated or overwhelmed by people, animals, microbes, or plants imported from foreign lands.

If they survive, native plants grow now in mountain retreats or in remote valleys untouched by progress. Notable among these products of evolution in isolation made only in Hawaii are the graceful *koa,* whose expanded, flat, crescent leaf-stem soon replaces the leaflets typical of acacias; the silversword, adapted to the alpine heights of Maui and Hawaii; the even rarer green-sword of Haleakala; handsome tree lobelias, whose flowers are curved to the shape of the beaks of the endemic birds which sipped their nectar. Many are beautiful, as these watercolors attest. They were painted in the 1880s by Mrs. Francis Sinclair, Jr., of Makaweli, Kauai.

left to right

'IE'IE, climbing screwpine, *Freycinetia arborea*

'OHI'A LEHUA, *Metrosideros collina* subsp. *polymorpha*

'UKI'UKI, *Dianella ensifolia*

Illustrations from Mrs. Francis Sinclair, Jr. 1885. "Indigenous Flowers of the Hawaiian Islands."

Hawaii's lush flora, like its people and its animals, is borrowed from almost everywhere else: 99 percent of the plants seen today upon our shores and plains are not native to Hawaii. Since 1778 almost 2,000 kinds of new plants have been introduced either intentionally or accidentally. Before 1850 most of those were food plants or weeds. Since that time ornamentals and forest trees have been favored. Many importations, such as the three kinds of guavas, Java plum, algaroba, lantana, Christmas berry, ironwood, silver oak, brassaia, tibouchina, bamboos and other grasses, even the graceful palms and fragrant gingers, have escaped from cultivation, to take conspicuous places in the Hawaiian landscape.

Before the foreigners arrived, with all their exotic plants, animals, textiles, tools, and machines, Hawaiians relied heavily upon the plants which Nature or their ancestors had established in the islands. Because they had no metals, no clay, no tools other than those they fashioned from stones, pieces of wood, or splinters of shell and bone, Hawaiians had learned to use plant materials in many ingenious ways. From one part or another of those plants they obtained shelter, clothing, tools, utensils, ornaments, dyes, light, medicines, as well as motifs in art and talismans to protect them from the magic of sorcerers or the wrath of the gods.

They had given names to herbs, shrubs, and trees, and classified them according to resemblances, real or fancied, to other familiar things. They cultivated fields or groves of edible plants, such as taro, sweet potato, breadfruit, banana, and coconut, gathered food from others, such as mountain apples and *kukui* nuts, wherever they grew. Plantations of the paper mulberry, or *wauke,* provided the bark from which women made *kapa.* 'Olona and *hau* gave the fibers from which men spun twine for fishnets and lashings, coconut husks the coarse material from which they made sennit.

Each of the seven kinds of indigenous plants illustrated here by Mrs. Sinclair's water colors yielded dyes, medicines, and either wood or thatch for shelters. The fruits of mountain apple, raspberry, and *noni* were edible, as were the aerial and underground tubers of the yam.

left to right (top)

NONI, *Morinda citrifolia*
UHI, yam, *Dioscorea alata*

left to right (bottom)

'AKALA, raspberry, *Rubus hawaiiensis*
'OHI'A 'AI, mountain apple, *Eugenia malaccensis*

59

Fishes

The ancestors of most marine plants and animals now found in Hawaii came from the warm, fecund Indo-Pacific seas. Although North America is closer, its coastal waters have contributed little to Hawaii's marine flora and fauna. Ocean currents and temperatures, the major factors affecting distribution of water-borne organisms, favored migrants from Indonesia or southeast Asia and blocked those from America. Ultimately many of the immigrants, forced to adapt to new environments as they wandered and after they reached this mid-Pacific habitat, evolved into the species which biologists consider to be indigenous to Hawaii. The numbers and kinds of reef and shore creatures differ with place, season, and depth. Oahu's shores retain a surprising assortment of both plants and animals, but less frequented beaches on neighbor islands are more rewarding. The ecology of a Hawaiian Reef is revealed most clearly in the exhibit at Sea Life Park.

left to right, top row

Scarus dubius
Antigonia steindachneri
Chaetodon trifasciatus

middle row

LAU'I-PALA, *Zebrasoma flavescens*
HUMUHUMU-'ELE'ELE, *Melichthys buniva*
LAU-WILIWILI-NUKUNUKU-'OI'OI,
   Forcipiger longirostris

bottom row

PAKU'IKU'I, *Acanthurus achilles*
PO'O-PA'A, *Cirrhitus alternatus*
NOHU, *Scorpaenopsis cacopsis*

The ocean has always been the primary source of edible fish for Hawaiians, because the islands lack extensive rivers and lakes. Ichthyologists have identified about 600 species more or less indigenous to Hawaiian waters, ranging in size from huge sharks to inconspicuous things smaller than the *humu* in *humuhumunukunukuapua'a*. New discoveries are made each year, as methods for collecting specimens in deeper waters are improved. Biologists in research submarines, while exploring the submerged slopes off western Oahu, have seen great numbers of marine creatures, both known and new to science, living in that fertile zone.

The state has established several undersea parks, with marked trails, for skin-divers and SCUBA-divers who prefer to look at fish rather than catch them. The deeper waters off the leeward coasts present sports-fishermen with record-breaking marlins, broadbills, sailfish, *mahimahi,* and tunas. Less energetic folk enjoy displays at Waikiki Aquarium and Sea Life Park.

left to right, top row

HUMUHUMU-NUKUNUKU-A-PUA'A,
　Rhinecanthus aculeatus
MALOLO, *Parexocoetus brachypterus*
Chaetodon miliaris

middle row

KIKIKAPU, *Holocanthus arcuatus*
PA'U'U, *Myripristis chryseres*
KIHIKIHI, *Zanclus canescens*

bottom row

Holotrachys lima
KALA, *Naso unicornis*
'O'ILI UWIWI, *Pervagor spilosoma*

Illustrations from David Starr Jordan and Barton W. Evermann. 1905. "The Aquatic Resources of the Hawaiian Islands."

Fruits and Vegetables

The diet of aboriginal Hawaiians was adequate but dull. For fruits they had only mountain apples in their short season, sugarcane, and bananas; for vegetables, only taro, breadfruit, sweet potatoes, yams, coconuts, *kukui* nuts, ti roots, some kinds of seaweeds and ferns. Foreigners realized from the beginning that, for everyone's sake, the islands' stock of food plants must be diversified. Captain Cook himself left seeds of pumpkins, melons, and onions at Niihau in 1778. By 1800, Hawaiian farmers had learned from Europeans how to "rear to perfection" watermelons, muskmelons, strawberries, oranges, and many of the Occident's vegetables. Indefatigable Don Marin introduced other vegetables and a variety of fruits now widespread: guavas, pineapples, limes, lemons, prickly pears, and mangoes.

Settlers from the Orient imported seeds or stocks of plants needed in preparing their favorite foods, or just to provide a taste of home: fruits like persimmon, lychee, Satsuma orange, dragon's eye, and pummelo; and such vegetables as daikon, won bok, gobo, dasheen, soybean, rice, bitter melon, and eggplant. Today an appetizing blend of foods and recipes from East and West is served in homes and restaurants.

PINEAPPLES Don Marin planted the first pineapples in 1813. The Smooth Cayenne variety, now the major crop for island plantations, was introduced in 1885.

LIMES and lemons of many varieties have been introduced, mostly from Asia, since Don Marin planted the first lime seedling in his vineyard in Honolulu.

GUAVA Don Marin introduced the guava, native to tropical America, about 1825. Its sour fruits yield superlative juice, jams, and jellies.

BREADFRUIT, originally from Malaysia, was brought to Pacific islands by migrating Polynesians. Well ripened breadfruit, baked or steamed, is a treat for gourmets.

MANGO In 1824 Captain John Meek of Honolulu brought Don Marin some "common" mango seedlings from Manila.

LITCHI The first litchi seedling from China was planted in Hawaii in 1873. Most delicious when fresh, the grape-like fruits can be preserved by freezing or drying.

YAMS True yams, *Dioscorea alata*, are rarely seen anymore, although Captain Cook bought them in quantities at Kauai and Niihau. Most "yams" sold in markets today are varieties of sweet potatoes.

SUGARCANE The first Hawaiians brought sugarcane with them from the central Pacific. Island plantations grow interspecific hybrids.

PAPAYA, native to tropical America, provides islanders' favorite breakfast fruit, and the enzyme papain, used in biological research and as a meat tenderizer.

BANANAS "The Fruit of Paradise," as Europeans called bananas, originated in India. Hawaiians grew about 50 varieties, few of which survive.

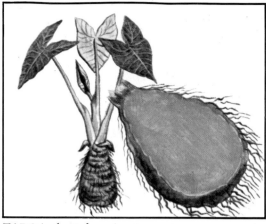

TARO is the Polynesians' most important starch-food. The cooked corms, pounded into a smooth paste and mixed with water, make *poi*. The tender leaves, called *luau*, are better than spinach.

PASSION FRUIT Although many species of passion fruit grow wild in Hawaii, only the yellow *liliko'i* is cultivated commercially. The complex flowers, whose parts symbolize the passion of Christ, give these plants their common name.

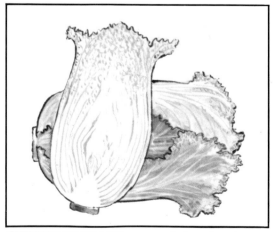

CHINESE CABBAGE, or won bok, prime ingredient in kim ch'i, was one of the first vegetables introduced from the Orient.

Holidays and Celebrations

1
MAKAHIKI DAY is observed by school children and Boy Scouts in November. Ancient Hawaii's Makahiki season was from October through January, when people met at friendly sports contests rather than upon a field of battle.

2
KAMEHAMEHA DAY If Hawaii were still a monarchy, June 11 would be our most important national holiday. Started almost a hundred years ago to honor Kamehameha I, it recalls now, in parades, pageants, luaus, hulas, and a climactic glittering grand ball, the glamour and the beauty of the lost Kingdom of Hawaii.

3
CHRISTMAS Everyone, regardless of race or creed, is caught up in the great commercial feast of Christmas. According to his whim, Santa Claus arrives by canoe, surfboard, jet plane, or helicopter, but never in a sled drawn by eight reindeer.

4
WESAK About the time when Occidentals celebrate Easter, Orientals celebrate the birthday of Buddha with Wesak or, as it is called in Japanese, Hanamatsuri, the Flower Festival.

5
CHINESE NEW YEAR (which, depending upon the moon, comes a month or so after that of the Western calendar) is greeted with fireworks, feasting, lion dancers, flowering narcissus plants, and delectable confections.

6
BOYS' DAY, for Japanese families, is May 5. Those heroic fish, flying like kites from a pole above a boy's home and symbolic of Japan's carp, are made of oiled paper or cloth, or nowadays of plastic. They are gifts from friends, urging him to heed the example of the strong, persevering carp. Girls have their "Doll Day" on March 3.

7
SAMOAN FLAG DAY is August 15, when the Samoan community commemorates America's annexation of eastern Samoa in 1900 with feasting, cultural exhibits, singing, and dancing.

8
BABY LUAU A happy custom, borrowed from party-loving Hawaiians, is the baby luau, presented in celebration of a child's first birthday.

9
MEMORIAL DAY The dead of all races and religions are honored on America's Memorial Day, May 30. Especially poignant are the ceremonies and the flowers for those who are buried in the National Memorial Cemetery of the Pacific, within Punchbowl's green, quiet crater.

10
BON ODORI Throughout the summer, especially in August, Japanese Buddhists remember the spirits of relatives who have died during the past year with somber rituals at temples and shrines, and with the happy dances of Bon Odori. At these gatherings which, with their food booths and resounding orchestras, resemble village fairs, relatives and spectators alike can join in the posturing dances.

11
LEI DAY Since 1928, "May Day Is Lei Day in Hawaii." This most endemic of Hawaii's festivals is neglected somewhat now in Honolulu, where leis are becoming more expensive. Residents in smaller communities, however, find time to make and to wear leis, and their children in school still present ceremonial pageants to entertain their Lei Queen and her court.

12
FLORES DE MAYO is a Filipino festival imported from the home country. Youths and maidens in Philippine costumes honor the Blessed Virgin Mary, Christian saints, and universal virtues with candle-lit processions, flowers, songs, and dances.

1

5

9

2

3

4

6

7

8

10

11

12

A Sampling of Local Expressions

Among themselves islanders communicate in a language loaded with words and phrases borrowed from their several parent cultures. Children learn these polyglot vocabularies as naturally as they acquire relatives and friends, or develop a taste for cokes, *sushi, see moi,* and TV. But *haoles* who want to use these quaint terms should select them with caution and pronounce them with care. Hawaiian words especially, rich in double- and triple-meanings or ribald improprieties, can be embarrasing traps for the uninstructed. Genuine pidgin-English, seldom spoken anymore, has been replaced by a debased dialect that employs English words sloppily pronounced, a syntax reduced to essentials, staccato speed, and swooping rhythms.

HAWAII NEI: all the islands in the group, to distinguish them from the Big Island of Hawaii alone.

HAOLE: in the old days, a foreigner from any land. Nowadays, the term applies only to Caucasians.

LEI HULU: *Leis* made of feathers, rare and costly even in olden times, were worn only by female chiefs of great rank.

KAPU: The Hawaiian form of that well-known word, taboo. Used as a noun, it means a rule or prohibition, or something forbidden; used as a verb (most often on signs) it means KEEP OUT.

SEE MOI: Chinese plums, soaked in brine, then dried. Undoubtedly the saltiest preserve known to man. A great selection of preserved fruits—crack-seed, mango-seed, sweet-sour seed, wet seed, dry seed, and a host of others—are imported from Hong Kong and Taiwan.

"GO FOR BROKE": Originally a playground colloquialism for "Do your best," during World War II this became the battle-cry of Hawaii's soldiers of Japanese ancestry as they fought their way to fame and glory in America's campaigns through Italy and France.

ZORI: Japanese flat sandals or slippers, formerly made of woven rice straw, now mass-produced in rubber. **GETA:** Japanese wooden clogs, with cross-pieces of wood 1 to 4 inches high. **TABI:** the Japanese sock, resembling a mitten more than a stocking.

SASHIMI is Japan's major contribution to Hawaii's *pupu* set: very thin slices of raw fish, served on a snow-white nest of crisp, cool *daikon.*

'OKOLE MALUNA: A literal (but vulgar) translation into Hawaiian of the drinkers' salute, "Bottoms up."

HUKILAU: If you're fortunate enough to be going to a *hukilau,* you'll be helping a lot of other folk to pull *(huki)* a dragnet *(lau)* to shore. By custom, the owner of the seine shares the catch with his helpers.

ULIULI (and watch your pronunciation!): those gourd rattles, topped with dyed feathers, which hula dancers shake so expertly.

KAUKAU: food of any kind. When it's delicious, the kaukau is ONO.

PAU: done, finished, ended. The one absolutely necessary Hawaiian word in every home.

PA'U: a skirt, which may be as brief as a mini or as voluminous as the colorful drapery worn by a "pa'u rider in the Kamehameha Day parade."

ALOHA: hello, goodbye, love, affection, regard, and how-do-you-do?

PUPU: Originally the Hawaiians' word for shells from sea or land; now almost exclusively reserved for hors d'oeuvres and cocktail-party snacks.

MU'UMU'U: deformed or shapeless, cut-off, maimed; a loose-fitting, shapeless dress which makes the wearer more so.

HOLOKU: a fitted dress, with a yoke and sometimes a train, similar to the Mother Hubbard.

MABUHAY: hello, or greetings, in Tagalog.

'HAWAIIAN TIME'': "a little bit late," anywhere from 5 minutes to 5 hours after the appointed time.

A'A: rough, fragmented lava; as opposed to *pahoehoe:* smooth, unbroken lava. The terms have been adopted by geologists throughout the world.

LAULAU: a package of food, wrapped in ti leaves, containing morsels of pork or beef and fish, enclosed in taro leaves.

SUSHI: cold rice with a core of pickled vegetables or fish; called "inarizushi" when stuffed into a cone of golden soybean curd (tofu), "makizushi" when rolled in cylinders enclosed in casings of dried black seaweed.

KAMAAINA: literally, "a child of the land," born and raised in Hawaii. A newcomer, or a guest, is a **MALIHINI.**

MENEHUNE: the first people to settle in these islands, probably smaller in body and darker of skin than later colonists from Polynesia.

MAUKA: toward the mountains. **MAKAI:** toward the sea. When giving directions, kamaainas refer to landmarks rather than to points of the compass. For example, in Honolulu, to reach Iolani Palace from Aloha Tower, "you go mauka four blocks, then waikiki three blocks."

LUAU: a native Hawaiian feast, so called because luau, taro leaves, usually cooked with coconut cream and pork or chicken, are a featured dish.

"SUCK 'EM UP": Usually pronounced "Sock 'um op," and generally (but not always) referring to alcoholic beverages, this can be a toast, an expletive, an invitation, or a cheering exhortation, depending upon speaker and circumstances.

PUA: A *pua* is a flower. A *pua'a* is a pig. A *luau* presents the nicest way for the twain to meet.

IMU: the Polynesian earth-oven, in which foods are cooked with heat released from hot rocks.

PALI: a cliff or precipice. "The Pali" is the one of Nuuanu, on Oahu.

DA KINE: a corruption of "that kind," a generalization used by people too lazy to think of the right word.

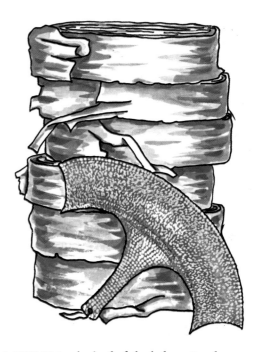

LAUHALA: the leaf of the hala or Pandanus tree. From these leaves, cleaned, stripped of their sawtooth edges, stored in rolls, Polynesians plait mats, purses, fans, coasters, hats, and other articles.

SHIBUI is the Japanese word for elegant simplicity. *Shibai* is their sneer for the false, the phony, the sham.

Fact and Fiction

Much of the fun of living in Hawaii comes from enjoying the inventions of imagination—that ecumenical assortment of myths, legends, superstitions, illusions, traditions, rumors, gossip, and fabrications, encrusted upon a few more or less discernible facts, around which we build our conversations and our attitudes.

We may pretend to scoff at those stories about Madame Pele's hitchhiking along the Big Island's highways, but not one of us dares to ignore a little old Tutu who's out thumbing a ride. We thrill to tales about the Marchers of the Night, to accounts of houses, cemeteries, or whole forests haunted by malevolent *kahuna 'ana'ana,* Japanese fox spirits, Chinese devils, or pallid English ghosts. We make the prescribed sacrifices to resident gods when we enter their silent fanes. We know that Pele lives: when she holds court in her fiery palace at Kilauea, we approach in awe, offering chants in praise of her, tribute in *'ohelo* berries, maile *leis,* and, more recently, bottles of anything alcoholic.

And, despite all evidence to the contrary, we cherish the most persistent myth of all: the belief that always, since first men found them, these islands have been green and lovely, undespoiled and unspoilable, inhabited by carefree happy people whose hearts are light, whose voices are lifted in song.

UKULELE Most people think that Hawaiians invented the ukulele. Actually, it is a local variant of the Portuguese cavaquinho, introduced by contract-laborers in the 1880s. Musical Hawaiians happily took it up, as earlier they had adopted the Spanish guitar.

CHINESE FIRECRACKERS scare devils and evil spirits from feasts, weddings, and funerals.

ALOE BARBADENSIS leaf sap (mispronounced "ah loy" by folk who think the name is Hawaiian) is used in treating burns, cuts, and skin infections.

GRASS SKIRT Neither is the grass skirt native to Hawaii. Hula dancers adopted it from Micronesian immigrants in the 1880s. Skirts made of ti leaves, cellophane, or plastic are later variations of that borrowed theme.

NUUANU PALI At the battle of Nuuanu in 1795, King Kamehameha did not push thousands of Oahu's defenders over the Pali. Only a few warriors jumped or fell into the abyss, preferring honorable death to being captured and sacrificed.

LAE AHI, cape of fire, was the Hawaiians' name for Diamond Head, probably because long ago signal beacons were lighted there, possibly because Hi'iaka, Pele's younger sister, compared it with the brow *(lae)* of the *'ahi* fish, the yellow-fin tuna. Foreign residents corrupted the term to Leahi. The *haole* name dates from 1825, when British sailors thought that Pele's tears formed in the mountain's lava were diamonds.

SACRED FALLS VALLEY, a narrow cleft in the Ko'olau Range near Hau'ula on Oahu, is a fine example of stream-erosion. According to legend, however, it was scored into the mountain by the cloven hoof of Kamapua'a, the mischievous pig god, when he leaped over the steep ridge to escape hunters he had angered. Kamapua'a still frequents the place; and wise people who enter his abode will placate him with sacrifices of leaves each time they cross the valley's little stream, if they don't want him to hurl rocks upon them from the high cliffs above.

KIM CH'I, or "Kim Chee" in Hawaii, a Korean dish, is a mouth-watering, belly-warming combination of salted, pickled Chinese cabbage and other vegetables, suffused with garlic and braced with chili peppers.

OHIA LEHUA "Plucking an *ohia lehua* blossom will bring rain," said the people of old. Usually the prophecy is fulfilled, because the *ohia lehua* trees grow best in rain country.

Suggested Reading

ABRAMSON, JOAN. 1976 *Photographers of Old Hawaii.* Honolulu: Island Heritage Limited.

ALLEN, GWENFREAD. 1950. *Hawaii's War Years.* Honolulu: University of Hawaii Press.

APPLE, RUSS and PEG. 1977. *Tales of Old Hawaii.* Honolulu: Island Heritage Limited.

BARROW, TERENCE. 1976. *Captain Cook in Hawaii.* Honolulu: Island Heritage Limited.

BERGER, ANDREW J. 1977. *The Exotic Birds of Hawaii.* Honolulu: Island Heritage Limited.

DAWS, A. GAVAN. 1968. *Shoal of Time.* New York: Macmillan.

DAY, A. GROVE, and CARL STROVEN. 1959. *A Hawaiian Reader.* New York: Appleton-Century-Crofts, Inc.

FEHER, JOSEPH. 1969. *Hawaii: A Pictorial History.* Honolulu: Bishop Museum Press.

FUCHS, LAWRENCE H. 1961. *Hawaii Pono: A Social History.* New York: Harcourt, Brace and World.

GOODMAN, ROBERT B., A. G. DAWS, and E. SHEEHAN. 1970. *The Hawaiians.* Honolulu: Island Heritage Limited.

GOSLINE, W. A., and VERNON BROCK. 1965. *Handbook of Hawaiian Fishes.* Honolulu: University of Hawaii Press.

HAWAII AUDUBON SOCIETY. 1967. *Hawaii's Birds.* Honolulu: Published by the Audubon Society.

I'I, JOHN PAPA. 1959. *Fragments of Hawaiian History.* Honolulu: Bishop Museum Press.

INOUYE, DANIEL K., with LAWRENCE ELLIOTT. 1967. *Journey to Washington.* Englewood Cliffs, N.J.: Prentice-Hall, Inc.

JORDAN, DAVID STARR, and BARTON W. EVERMANN. 1905. *The Aquatic Resources of the Hawaiian Islands.* Washington, D.C.: Bulletin, United States Fish Commission, Volume XXIII for 1903.

JUDD, G. P., IV. 1961. *Hawaii, an Informal History.* New York: Colliers.

KAMAKAU, SAMUEL M. 1964. *Ka Po'e Kahiko: The People of Old.* Honolulu: Bishop Museum Press.

KANE, HERB KAWAINUI. 1976. *Voyage: The Discovery of Hawaii.* Honolulu: Island Heritage Limited.

KRAUSS, BOB. 1977. *Island Way.* Honolulu: Island Heritage Limited.

————. 1978. *Kauai.* Honolulu: Island Heritage Limited.

KORN, ALFONS. 1958. *The Victorian Visitors.* Honolulu: University of Hawaii Press.

KUYKENDALL, RALPH S. 1938, 1953, 1967. *The Hawaiian Kingdom.* Vol. I, 1778-1854, Foundations and Transformation. Vol. II, 1854-1874, Twenty Critical Years. Vol. III, 1874-1893, The Kalakaua Dynasty. Honolulu: University of Hawaii Press.

LIND, ANDREW. 1968. *Hawaii's People.* Honolulu: University of Hawaii Press.

LOOMIS, ALBERTINE. 1951, 1966. *Grapes of Canaan.* Honolulu: Hawaiian Mission Children's Society.

MACDONALD, GORDON A., and AGATIN ABBOTT. 1970. *Volcanoes in the Sea.* Honolulu: University of Hawaii Press.

NEAL, MARIE C. 1965. *In Gardens of Hawaii.* Honolulu: Bishop Museum Press.

PUKUI, MARY KAWENA, and SAMUEL H. ELBERT, 1966. *Place Names of Hawaii.* Honolulu: University of Hawaii Press.

ROTHSCHILD, WALTER. 1893-1900. *The Avifauna of Laysan and the Hawaiian Possessions.* London: R. H. Porter.

SCHMITT, ROBERT C. 1968. *Demographic Statistics of Hawaii, 1778-1965.* Honolulu: University of Hawaii Press.

SINCLAIR, MRS. FRANCIS, JR. 1885. *Indigenous Flowers of the Hawaiian Islands.* London: Sampson Low, Marston, Searle, and Rivington.

STEARNS, HAROLD T. 1966. *Geology of the State of Hawaii.* Palo Alto, California: Pacific Books.

STONE, SCOTT C. S. 1977. *Pearl Harbor: The Way it Was.* Honolulu: Island Heritage Limited.

————. 1977. *Volcano!!* Honolulu: Island Heritage Limited.

TITCOMB, MARGARET. 1963. *The Voyage o the Flying Bird.* New York: Dodd, Mead.

WENKAM, ROBERT. 1967. *Kauai and the Par Country of Hawaii.* Sierra Club.

WILSON, S. B., and A. H. EVANS. 1890-1899 *Aves Hawaiienses.* London: R. H. Porter.